GUS GEORGE ANGELOS

AN AUTOBIOGRAPHY

Gus G. Angelos

GUS GEORGE ANGELOS

AN AUTOBIOGRAPHY

Gus G. Angelos

Doce Blant Publishing

www.DoceBlantPublishing.com

Published by Doce Blant Publishing, Dana Point, CA 92629

www.doceblantpublishing.com

Cover by Fiona Jayde Media

ISBN: 978-0-9967622-9-8

Printed in the United States of America

Table of Contents

Introduction

B oyd K. Packer, President of the Council of the Twelve of the Church of Jesus Christ of Latter Day Saints Church stated, at a general priesthood session, "Old men look to the past because they have no future. Young men look to the future because they have no past."

I am seventy-three years old and this is my life story, written in 2003 with later updates. I regret that I didn't keep a good journal all my life. It is my hope that whoever reads this will find it interesting, learn something, and be better off for the time spent in learning how I traveled throughout life, during my time in history. My life has truly been a marvelous, wonderful experience. When my time comes to leave this mortal existence, know that I have been greatly blessed with the best things life had to offer: namely, a secure and happy childhood with decent and wonderful parents, a great wife and family, a wonderful religion, a free country with unlimited opportunity to follow my dreams, and a great profession; (Orthodontics, which allowed me to help many people and enjoy a nice standard of living).

I was able to choose a wonderful area in which to live. An added bonus was to have good health, and live during a time in history where things changed and developed so fast. Many great events of the world took place during my time. During the month I was born, the Stock Market crashed and the Great Depression started. The Depression and World War II lasted until I was sixteen. This was a time when radio was the main form of entertainment. Most households had one radio. A few families had a phonograph player. Talking movies had only been around for a few years. Television was still twenty years away, and computers and electronic items were forty plus years in the future. Photographs were taken only on special occasions because of the expense. Many households didn't even have a camera. People had 'ice boxes' rather than refrigerators, and homes were heated with coal stoves or furnaces. Central heating and air conditioners were for the future. Life was simpler and events moved slower.

Growing up was much safer then. It has been a remarkable time to live in, though it has had some great challenges. I have enjoyed a long happy life. I have endeavored to write my life story as accurately as possible. I hope that I haven't exaggerated. We all know that life isn't fair and that everyone has their 'ups and downs'. That is just the way life is. Have I made mistakes? Yes, I made my share, but I always learned from them. I would also like it to be known that I always tried to give it (life and goals) my best shot (effort).

The Lord gave me many gifts, which included persistence and grit to follow my dreams and goals. I had lots of luck and help along the way, especially from my wife Pearl. The bottom line is, the Lord has been very good to me.

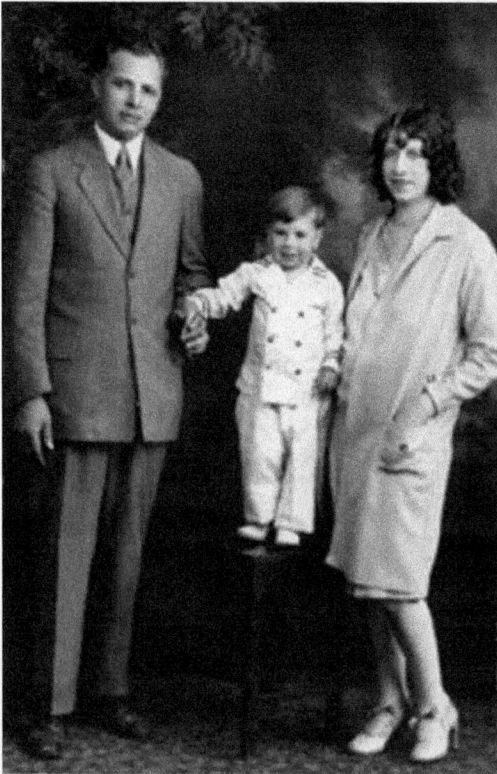

Dad, Sam, Pregnant Mom 1929

Here is the family I was born into: I am a first generation American. I was born in Salt Lake City, Utah on October 3, 1929 at 12:51 p.m. in the Holy Cross Hospital as the second of three children. I weighed 10 ½ pounds. No record was kept as to how long I was at birth. The location of the hospital is 100 South and 1000 East and it is now called Salt Lake Regional Medical Center.

My father's name was George Sam Angelos, and he was thirty-five years old when I was born. My mother's name was Elsie Katy Bertha Waterman, and she was twenty-two years old when I was born. My father was born in Akrata, Greece on May 6, 1893. He immigrated to this country in 1911. My mother was born in Brunswick, Germany on February

An Autobiography

15, 1907. She immigrated to this country in about 1913. My parents were married on February 12, 1926 in Salt Lake. They met when my father hired my mother as a waitress in the first cafe he owned. I don't know how long they knew each other before they got married. My first home was the Santa Ana Apartment located on about 300 South and 400 East in Salt Lake City, Utah. The building has been torn down. My parents bought a home at 127 Harvard Avenue sometime around 1931. I do not remember the move to Harvard Avenue, as I was about two years of age. But I lived on Harvard Ave. until I went to the University of Wyoming and got married.

That Salt Lake City neighborhood was a nice middle class area to grow up in that had lots of children there. During the 1930's, the USA had the Great Depression when 25% of the people could not find work and economic times were extremely difficult. Federal and State welfare programs were pretty much non-existent at that time.

My earliest memory was visiting my great grandfather and great grandmother, Matern in Poplar Grove on the west side of Salt Lake. I only remember visiting them one time. They had a dog that did tricks. I thought the dog was smarter than me because I couldn't understand the commands for the dog to sit up, roll over, shake hands and things like that, which were given in German. I also remember my great grandfather's funeral and women crying and the casket on canvas strips ready to be lowered into the ground. No photographs were taken of that event. We didn't talk about it. So that is truly my earliest memory. Great grandfather died in February, 1932 when I was three years and four months old.

My mother's grandparents, the Materns emigrated from Germany around 1909. They were parents to eleven boys and one girl. The girl became my mother's mother. My great grandfather Matern became a U.S. citizen and I was told my great grandmother automatically had become a citizen, being the wife of a citizen. I don't think that was the law in those days, but I have never checked it out to be certain.

My great grandmother never learned to speak English and lived to be ninety-four years old. I was never able to get to know her very well due to the language problem and didn't see her very often. She was a short, jolly, nice woman.

The Matern Family immigrated to this country because of the Mormon Church. When they emigrated, two sons stayed in Germany and never emigrated or traveled to the U.S.A. After my mother died, her half sister Annie told us that my grandmother was left in Germany as punishment when dad, Sam, Mom who was pregnant, all emigrated to the U.S. in1929. I was told Grandmother Bertha was engaged to a man and got pregnant. They didn't get married and my mother was born out of wedlock.

Mom didn't tell me about this until I was thirty years old. The circumstance was a big stigma to mother. I believe being illegitimate had a profound effect on my mother's life. I think some family members blamed mom for bringing shame to the family.

My grandmother married Emil Waterman in Germany. He was not my mom's biological Father. Emil had to adopt my mother before they could immigrate to this country. I am not sure, but I think Mom was only five years old when she came to this country. Emil was a very mean man and was an alcoholic. I only remember seeing him once as a young boy, but I was afraid of him. Mother told us stories of being beaten with a belt by Emil, and of having to polishing his boots. She told us how if she stayed to play late, Emil would ride his bike to her school and make her come home. Mom spoke of another time when Emil was intoxicated, fired a gun through the ceiling, and the bullet almost hit somebody upstairs.

When Emil Waterman died around 1980, only mother and Emil's daughter Annie attended the funeral. Mom said her grandparents treated her very well. Her grandmother was the person who told mom when she was about twelve years of age that Emil wasn't her real father. A few years later, mom upset everyone by taking out an ad in the classified section of the newspaper, asking publically where her biological father could be located. No one responded.

My grandmother eventually divorced Emil Waterman and married Tony Floor, who I remember during my early years. They lived in Tooele, Utah most of the time. My grandmother wanted us children to call her 'Nanny' because she didn't think she looked old enough to be a grandmother. I didn't like the idea as a little kid but went along with it most of the time. Nanny eventually had two more husbands. She really got along well with men. She was a pleasant and attractive woman. She would come to Salt Lake on occasion and she and my mother would talk for long periods of time in German.

Mother was forced to quit school when she was twelve and go to work with her mother, cleaning houses. About the age of fourteen, mom started to work as a waitress. Eventually, she got a waitress job, working for my father at the Commercial Café. My sister and I think our mother was physically and probably sexually abused as a child, growing up. We have no proof, but we think mom was shy and would have been an easy target.

After mom died at age eighty-five, her half sister, Annie Muir told us that our mother had been married in Elko, Nevada for a short time. This marriage took place when my mother was very young. Mom and her husband lived in poverty in a hotel in Salt Lake. Grandmother took the lead in getting an annulment according to Aunt Annie. My nephew, Rob Forsgren looked up the marriage record in Elko when he was on a business trip and found the marriage record. I believe mom got married to get away from home. Mom bought her mother a piano before she got married. That must have been a big sacrifice.

Mom had two half brothers named George and Fred, and a half sister named Annie. Uncle Fred Waterman was a nice cheerful man

Grandmother Bertha, Great Grandmother Matern Mom & Sister Margaret - Four Generations

who had an artificial leg. He lost his leg as a teenager. While sleeping over night at a friend's house, a monkey stove, used to heat water, blew up and a piece of shrapnel lodged in his leg. Infection set in and the leg was amputated to save his life. This was at a time when antibiotics and sulfa drugs had not been discovered. Freddie, as we called him, became a barber but was a heavy drinker and died at the age of thirty-six from liver damage caused by the alcoholism. He lived with us for a while and could play the accordion, guitar, and sing pretty well. He was married for a short time but never had any children.

　　We hardly ever saw Uncle George Waterman, the oldest. He got married a couple of times and had some children we never got to know. He even started a Church of some kind in California. As we grew up, mother's brothers seldom visited us and I think when they did come by the house they usually wanted money or some kind of help. Times were tough and mother was always generous. Mom's half-sister, Annie married very early to get away from home as well. She married Albert Hoffman and lived in Tooele. After five boys and twenty years of marriage, she divorced him. Albert was an alcoholic and was a poor provider. Annie eventually married a nice fellow named Millard Muir. They had one more boy, who had had lots of troubles with drugs and the law. The other boys turned out pretty good, although two died quite young. We never got very well acquainted with Aunt Annie's boys because they lived in Tooele. Aunt Annie died at about the same age as mother – eighty-five years old. George Waterman died in his seventies.

Mom about 1925

Two of my mother's uncles on the Matern side lived close to us and some of their children were about the same ages as Sam, Margaret, and me. We saw the kids at school and a couple of times we went to Saltair Resort with them. They were all good kids.

　　With dad's work and mom's health problems, we didn't ever visit anyone or have family reunions, parties, or things of that nature. Mother was a real people person. She was not an early riser and wasn't much of a "go get them" type of person. Mom was about five feet two inches tall and generally weighed between 120 and 135 pounds as I was growing up. She was a pretty woman and had blue eyes and had reddish hair, which she usually colored blonde. We, her children, think she did a good job raising us, especially with dad being away at work most of the time.

An Autobiography

I have pretty good genealogy records on my mom's Matern line. Pearl and I have tried to get everything together for genealogical records on my side, but the Greek line is extremely difficult. All the information about my dad's family has come from mom's relatives living in Greece, some of whom are now dead. I have written the Greek Orthodox Church headquarters in Athens, Greece as well as the local Greek Church in Akrata. I have inquired about records at the local city and county offices in Akrata, Greece. I was told they had no records. An American-Greek genealogy lady, who was raised in Greece, also told me that there are records but the authorities will not cooperate. Evidently legal and court battles over orphans and adoptions dating back to World War II are the problem. I hope conditions will change in the future. I have been to the LDS Church Family History Library a few times, but I have not been able to obtain any information to date. Pearl and I have pretty much taken the lead to obtain family history, as my brother and sister have not been very interested in genealogy. The records we do have were obtained from family members in Greece.

Dad's life was different. He immigrated to the U.S.A. in 1911 at the age of eighteen. His older brother Tony immigrated first in 1910, followed by dad, and then Uncle Nick in 1917. Uncle Bill Angelos of Pocatello, who I think was a second cousin to my dad, came before Uncle Tony. They all emigrated to seek out opportunities they didn't have and find a better life. Dad's first job was with the Union Pacific in Las Vegas, Nevada. A short time later he moved to Salt Lake City and got a job with the Pullman Car Company, which made deluxe railroad passenger cars. Dad said he got to be boss over a few men. After a few years, he bought a restaurant (Commercial Café) in Salt Lake on 2nd South and Regent Street. That is where he hired my mother as a waitress.

Dad lost the restaurant in 1932 during the Great Depression. Dad's citizenship paper, which I have, is dated 1935. It says he was five feet ten inches tall and weighed 185 pounds. We have very few pictures of our Parents when they were young or during early marriage. Dad was a nice looking man. He never mastered the English language but did fine with a typical Greek accent. He was a good businessman – very intelligent and a very hard worker. You have to give a great deal of credit to immigrates like my dad, who came to the U.S.A., didn't speak English, and were able to have a business of their own in just a few years. As a young boy in Greece, he was only able to attend school for two years – the first and second grades. That was the extent of his formal education. The family was poor and the boys were allowed two years of school while the girls did not receive any schooling at all. I was told there was no free education in rural areas in those days, so the family did the best they could. The village population was about 2,000.

In 1958, I went to Akrata, Greece. The village had changed very little, situated in the country, and still very small. I met my Uncle John, who had been the mayor of the village, and my Aunt Pariescavie. My aunt never learned to read or write. All of the Greek family members were, and are, members of the Greek Orthodox Church. The brothers in America sent money back to the "Old Country" during most all their lives. The men all smoked and emanated the Greek culture through and through.

All of the relatives in Greece are wonderful people. They have always treated us like royalty. All of the Greek cousins in my age group, as well as their children, are college educated and seem to be doing well. Sam, Margaret, and I, along with our cousin Richard Angelos, and our spouses, visited our Greek relatives in 1998 and had a wonderful visit. We rarely correspond with our Greek relatives. Both Sam and I have our dad's first name as our middle name. This is the Greek tradition. The first son in a family has the grandfather's first name as his first name, and the father's first name as his middle name. The additional boys born into the family will have their father's first name as their middle name. Therefore both Sam and I have George for our middle name.

When my dad emigrated to the U.S., his last name was shortened from Angelotopolous to Angelos. Evidently Angelopolous is a very common name in Greece. However, the 't' in our name's spelling, Angelatopolous is correct, according to Uncle Nick who spelled it on my Father's grave marker. My parents, Uncle Nick, Grandmother Bertha, Sam's godfather John Athens, and Emil Waterman are buried next to each other in Mount Olivet Cemetery in Salt Lake City. My great grandparents, the Materns, are buried in the City Cemetery in Salt Lake. Both my dad's parents died in Greece before I was born. I think they are buried in Akrata. I also think the grave areas are reused after a certain number of years.

Early Memories

Dad (2nd from right) 2 Brothers 2 Cousins on right. Photo taken about 1910

One of my other earliest memories was of milk in bottles, being delivered by a horse drawn wagon. I thought the horse was very smart because he would walk to the next house and stop without the milkman directing him. It was the first time I'd ever seen a horse. During the winter a horse drawn plow would clear the snow from the sidewalks. I thought that would be a great job for me when I grew up.

We had a screened-in front porch when I was very young. I remember one night on the porch when my mother had me on her lap and she showed me the moon. She said it was called a 'quarter moon'. I asked where the nickel moon was and everyone got a big laugh out of that. A nickel was something I could relate to. A quarter was too much money and I was too young to think in terms of a circle. I knew nothing of the phases of the moon.

Another early memory was when my father did not have a job. Before I was born, dad had a restaurant called the Commercial Café located on 2nd South and Regent Street in downtown Salt Lake. Things went along well until the Great Depression hit the USA and then dad lost the restaurant. It was in 1932. I remember getting up early in the morning when only my father and I were awake. My father would leave home to look for a job. It seemed like this took place over the summer in about 1933. Each day when he came home, I would ask if he found a job. He could see my concern and would laugh and tell me not to worry. It was probably a short time that this went on, but I remember being very worried. I believe this had a profound influence on me to be a saver of money rather than a spender. It starting with early childhood and exists to this day. I have always wanted to have financial security.

My dad did get a job at Latches Café which was located about 340 South Main Street in Salt Lake. Many years later, the Latches Café became the China Village Restaurant, which lasted thirty or forty years. My dad's job was that of a cook or chef. He worked the next twelve and a half years, every day of the year. He never had a single day off for illness, vacations, holidays, or anything. Dad would go to work about 7:00 a.m. He would come home from 4:15pm to 5:15 p.m., read the paper, take a short nap sitting in his favorite soft chair with his feet elevated on a footstool, and then go back to work. He would return home at about 10:30 p.m. Dad always rode the bus to and from work.

When dad would come home in the afternoon, mother would tell us to play outside, at a friends' house, or in the basement when it was cold because dad needed to rest. I remember when dad's teeth were removed and he got dentures. He had an ice pack on his jaw that afternoon, but he didn't miss work. Because of the long hours at work, I was unable to spend time with my father and this was a great tragedy for me. I had great love for him but didn't get to know him very well. Dad worked extremely hard and sacrificed everything, including his health, for the family. I never fully appreciated all he did for us when I was young.

After I graduated from high school, I did have an opportunity to know Dad better when Sam and I worked as waiters at his lunch stand. That was for about six months. He was a kind, patient man, who worked hard. He never had any hobbies or activities that I knew of. I think the only enjoyment for him was his family and work. He did enjoy talking to some regular customers at the restaurant. Many years after we left home, mom and dad played cards with neighborhood friends once a week. My mother had lots of health problems when I was young. She enjoyed better health as the years passed.

An Autobiography

My only brother, Sam was born May 12, 1927. He was a very good brother and I tagged along with him all of the time. My only sister, Margaret was born December 6, 1932. All of us children were baptized as infants in the Greek Orthodox Church in Salt Lake City. Sam's Greek Godfather, John Athens lived with us for a time and helped around the house. My mother's half brother, Fred Waterman also lived with us for a while. My Greek godfather went back to Greece while I was still very young. I don't remember him.

Margaret had a Godfather and a Godmother. I remember at times they would bring her presents for Christmas and special occasions. The purpose of a Godfather, as I understand it, is to generally look after the child, including his spirituality. Usually, the Godparent was a close family friend or relative.

Most of the time when we were not in school, Sam and I were pretty much left on our own to play with the many boys who lived on our street. There were generally about eight boys around the same ages as Sam and me. As I recall, Sam took me to school on my first day in kindergarten because my mom wasn't feeling well. We always walked to school together. The neighborhood was safe and had little traffic in those days.

Mom and Dad at Commercial Cafe

About half the families on our street owned a car. We did not have a car until I was almost sixteen years old. It was a real treat just to ride in a car in my early years. This only happened on rare occasions because we didn't have any close family friends or relatives. At times, I wished we had had some family friends or relatives to do special things with. About the only contact we had with adults was with the teachers in school. We didn't have church friends or activities, nor were there any community programs that we knew about.

Liberty Park was a half-mile away and there were playground swings and slides there. We went to Liberty Park in the summertime as we got older. Sam and I rode our bicycles when
we had to go very far away. Once in a while, we would ride the bus to town. This was not often.

Mom did take us to the State Fair three or four times when we were young. We also went to Lagoon and Saltair Resorts on the electric train a time or two. The only place we ever went as a family was to the Easter Midnight Mass at the Greek Orthodox Church, which was on 3rd South and 3rd West. It was always very crowded and most the time there was nowhere for us to sit. The chanting in Greek, the smell of incense, and late hour made it an unpleasant experience for me. It seemed as if the services took forever.

Once we had returned home, we would have a nice lamb dinner and break Easter eggs. We also rode in a taxi to and from church. The taxi ride was big treat. It is hard to remember, but I think we only did that for four or five years.

Due to my dad's work schedule, we never had meals together except at Thanksgiving when we ate during the hour that our dad was home. Other than that, we never went to a movie, took a ride in a car, had a vacation, or did anything together as a family. The only exception was a time or two during a few summers when Dad would take the 5th-East bus on his afternoon break to meet us all at Liberty Park. Mother would make a nice picnic lunch and put it in Sam's wagon and then we would walk to Liberty Park. Mother would play a little tennis or catch with us. Liberty Park was a fun place to go. There were lots of swings and slides to play on. It has really changed and been improved over the past seventy years. Dad was happy to sit on the blanket and enjoyed being together while he rested. This took place only a few times when we were very young during the summer.

One time, I remember as a very young boy, Sam would not include me in a game of catch he was playing with his older friends. Mother, as all good moms do, helped me learn to catch a ball. Mom enjoyed sports and was good at them, especially during that time when women and girls rarely had any interest in sports. This was during a time when schools did not offer any sports programs for girls.

A funny thing happened once when I was quite young. It was very unusual for mother to leave the house. If she did leave, she always took Margaret. We didn't have a telephone at that time. While Sam and I were home alone, a man came to the door and said if our parents didn't pay the water bill, the water company would shut off our water. Sam and I quickly filled up all of the glasses, jars, pots, and buckets that we could find with water. We thought we were saving the day. My parents really thought that was funny. I couldn't figure out the humor at that age.

I remember another incident about my mother's big heart and compassion. My mom was as kind and generous as anyone who has lived. I am sure many people would say the same about their mothers, but believe it or not, that is a true statement for me. A family named Steel that had five small children lived on our street. Their father was killed, I think in an auto accident. My mother and the three of us, as children, went to the Safeway store on the corner. She bought five big sacks of groceries for two dollars, which was a large amount of money during the depression. When it was dark, Sam and I were told to take the wagon with the groceries and put the five sacks on the front porch, ring the bell, and hide. We watched as they took the groceries into the house. It was very similar to the Valentine's Day deliver-then-hide occurrence, but a much more rewarding experience. It was customary in those days for kids to take a valentine to their friend's house, put the valentine on the porch, ring the bell, and then hide to watch for someone to pick up the valentine. Sometimes you would put a string on the valentine and pull it away as your friend started to pick it up. I think I must have been about seven or eight years old at the time of the grocery delivery. It was typical of my mom to like everyone and do kind deeds for everyone.

During the Great Depression, quite a few transients or 'hobos' as they were called in those days, would specifically come to our home and ask for food. There were railroad tracks three block from our house. I think the men probably passed along information to others about where they could get free food. Mom always fed them. We would take the food to the men in our back yard.

The men stopped coming when World War II started and jobs became available to everyone. The country completely mobilized in a united effort to win the war. There was never any opposition or protests to World War II. What could one say when the U.S.A. was suddenly attacked and then war declared on the United States by Japan and Germany? That is probably the only time in our country's history when there wasn't any opposition or protests to a war. It is also the only time our country completely mobilized for war. Remarkable things took place.

Sixteen to eighteen million people were called into the armed forces and the country manufactured hundreds of thousands of tanks, airplanes, and all the necessary things to win that war. The war items produced in this country were used by all the Allies, none of whom who had anything close to the industrial might of the USA. Many items were rationed and not available for civilian use during that time, but no one complained. Children like me collected scrap metal and bought war bonds and stamps to help out. We grew up thinking all wars were like that. As I learned more about American history, it turns out there has been significant opposition to all the wars involving the U.S.A. except World War II. There may have been a very small amount of opposition but at my age, I never knew of any.

Some time in the middle 1930's, Mother sang for a while in the Mormon Tabernacle Choir. To my knowledge, it was the only time she did something in the LDS Church. She was a room mother once for my class at Liberty School. She was also a room mother for Sam and Margaret's classes. Mother had outstanding talents for music, painting figurines, sewing, and making bed spreads and table cloths – things like that. She did a good job playing the piano and accordion by ear and had a nice singing voice. She won third place at the State Fair for being so fast at crocheting, and had a nice picture and article published in the Tribune newspaper as a result. Mother was a very good homemaker and had lots of skills that were needed to make things during her generation. She wasn't very good at technical school subjects.

Mom had a big heart and was good to everybody, especially her children. We loved her very much. She had a very difficult childhood but survived and always treated her mother and everyone else very well. Both mother and dad seemed to show love by giving material things. I never heard my dad tell any of us children that he loved us, but we knew he did. My mother was always there for us, and we knew she loved us. Mom was a homebody and didn't go many places. Everybody seemed to like our dad, although not many people knew dad very well because he worked so many hours each day. Anyone who met mom really liked her. I consider myself very fortunate to have been born and raised by two wonderful parents. I have always felt short changed by not being able to spend much time with my dad. I didn't get to know him very well. I think the total amount of time ever spent (just he and myself together) would be less than eight hours during the entire time I was growing up. Dad just worked all the time to give us a better life than he had. He made a real sacrifice to provide for the family at the costs of his time and health. I didn't appreciate the extent of this until I was much older.

It was very common in those days to pass clothes, toys, and things from older siblings to the younger children. It was the Great Depression time and everyone did it. Clothes were always patched, worn out, and then used for rags. When we got a hole in the sole of our shoes, a piece of cardboard was often put inside the shoe and we continued to wear them, especially in the summer. Sometimes, our parents would buy a shoe repair kit and glue new soles onto our shoes. But the soles usually ended up coming loose and you would walk along and flip the loose end under the shoe with each step. I didn't mind any of those experiences because it was that way for everyone in our neighborhood.

I got Sam's cloths as he outgrew them. Margaret, being the only girl got new items. In those days, families had one radio for entertainment. Books and magazines for children were hard to come by. Television, stereos, computers, iPods, and video games had not been invented. To see an airplane fly in the sky was even a pretty big deal. Life was simple. Kids played kick the can, hide and seek, Washington poke, rubber guns, and things like that. Roller-skates, ball games (sometimes with any ball you could find), and a stick for a bat were our pastimes. We threw rocks at tin cans or bottles or anything. We blew beans from cottonwood trees through a small piece of neon tube. We climbed trees, picked the beans, and obtained the neon tube from the trashcans belonging to sign companies. We flew kites, and built model airplanes when we could get money for those things. Children created things to do in those days – like smashing tin cans on your shoes.

Store bought toys were hard to come by so we made toys as best we could. Wooden boxes were available from the grocery store trash areas. We made lots of things from the wooden boxes. We were lucky and enjoyed a carefree childhood with many children on our block. You were safe and people didn't really have to lock their doors. There wasn't much traffic so we played in the streets close to home or went to the school playground. Going to Liberty Park was a long way to travel as a child. We were taught to ask permission from our mother when we left the block. We grew up happy.

Gus Estimate 3 years old

One scary event happened during my early childhood. It was unusual for anyone to move from our neighborhood. During one summer a family moved and the house was vacant for a period of time. I suppose I was six or seven years old. Sam, the two Safrin boys, along with me, found a basement window that was not locked in the vacant house. We made an agreement with Bruce Blake who was older than Sam that we would hide in the house and he would come and find us. We went into the vacant house and found what we thought would be the best hiding place. This was a small linen closet in the hall. Sid Safrin and I got on the top shelf because we were the smallest and the 2 bigger boys got on the bottom shelf. It was very crowded. We closed the door and the latch clicked. We waited for Bruce to come. After what seemed like a long time and no Bruce, we started hollering for Bruce to come and let us out. It got hot and stuffy locked inside the cabinet and it started to get hard to breath. We really got scared and I was afraid we would suffocate and die. We finally decided to break the door and all four of us started hitting the door at the same time to get out. After several hits, the latch came loose and we were able to get out. I always remembered that incident and after that experience, used more caution and better judgment when playing.

When I was nine years of age, the first tragedy involving any of my friends took place. A family named Jensen lived three houses from me. As I walked to school one day, I noticed a fire truck and police car parked in front of their house. This was the only time I remember any emergency vehicles on our street and it was exciting. After school my Mom told me that carbon monoxide gas had escaped from a faulty heater and had killed Donnie Jensen, who was an only child, and his mother. The dad was rescued in time to save his life.

Six of the neighborhood boys including Sam and I were asked to be Pall Bearers at the funeral of our friend who was six years old. I didn't like the experience. It was the second funeral I had ever gone went to – the first being my great grandfather's.

Early School Years

I went to Liberty Elementary School from kindergarten through sixth grade. My earliest memory of school was the first day of kindergarten. As mentioned earlier, I think Sam took me. I was still four years of age and remember the first time I needed to go to the restroom. I was very bashful and afraid to ask the teacher for permission. I finally went in my pants with the big one. I adjusted things and sat on the side of my chair. We had small chairs and were sitting in a circle. Some of the other children complained of an odor, and I tried to look very innocent. Nevertheless, I was very embarrassed. Mother handled the situation just fine when I got home and told me how to go about things in the future.

We made Mickey Mouse dolls that year. I kept mine for many years. We went to school for a half-day and would take a nap on a mat. I enjoyed school. Miss Taylor and Miss Empee were the kindergarten teachers. Kindergarten in those days was to prepare the children for first grade. It was in the first grade where children started learning how to read and write.

I had a rather difficult time in the early grades of school. I was the youngest in the class and didn't take any work home. I don't remember that much homework was ever assigned. The school furnished all the books and I don't think we were allowed to take home any schoolbooks.

Homework wasn't part of our family routine, as mother's health wasn't too good and she was usually busy being a good homemaker. I never remember my mother reading children stories or nursery rhymes to us. Unfortunately both sides of my family had little schooling and weren't able to supplement our formal schooling at home. My dad just worked all the time and mom had her hands full. On rare occasions, I remember my mother helping me with spelling words when the teacher sent home a word list that I was doing poorly with. Spelling was my hardest subject in grade school. To this day, I still am not good at spelling. I wanted to be in the top reading group in the early grades but was never good enough.

Kindergarten Class 1934

A very pivotal incident took place at school in the fourth grade. A math teacher, Miss Martin was getting acquainted with a new class in the fall. She gave us math problems to solve, and when we had the answer we would raise our hands. I got frustrated because most everyone was solving the problems quicker than I. Finally, I looked up a couple of the answers in the back of the textbook and raised my hand, so I could be recognized and tell the class the correct answer. Miss Martin did call on me and I gave the correct answer. Shortly after, she walked by my desk and saw I had only written down the problem and the answer. I didn't have any figures to show how I got the answer. She asked me how I got the answer and I told her that I just figured it out in my head. The problems were fairly difficult multiplication and division problems. I realized that Miss Martin knew I couldn't work the problems out in my head. I was expecting her to humiliate me in front of the whole class and was scared to death. It was one month before my ninth birthday, and I was shy and wanted to crawl under my desk and be invisible.

An Autobiography

Instead of reading me the riot act and embarrassing me in front of the class, Miss Martin eventually gave an assignment to the class and then came and sat with me at my desk. She told me she knew I couldn't work those problems out in my head. She spoke quietly and I admitted that I had looked in the back of the book for the answer. She then proceeded to tell me that if I worked hard, she thought I could be one of the better math students in the class. I have always wondered where Miss Martin got that idea.

My brother Sam had been in her class two years before, but I don't think he was outstanding. Sam was smart, but I think he tended to be lazy at times. I remember at least once, a teacher wrote on his report card that Sam was capable of doing better.

I did work hard with my studies and before the end of the forth grade, and from then on, I was one of the best math students at Liberty School. Math became my favorite subject and Miss Martin was my favorite teacher. Many times as I got older, I wished I would have gone back to Liberty School and told her how much she had helped me. I had a few outstanding teachers, but unfortunately didn't appreciate them until I was much older and more mature. Teaching is such a noble profession. It is too bad they aren't respected more and paid better.

Our classes in grade school were very big. We always had between thirty-seven and forty-five students. That experience in the fourth grade was the first time I remember any adult in an authoritative position giving me real encouragement. My mom was always great, but I never remember her telling me I could be good with schoolwork.

I went to Lincoln Junior High School for three years. Both my first two schools have since been torn down. Liberty School was rebuilt and renamed Lincoln Elementary. A small shopping mall is now on the property where Lincoln school was torn down. The school was on 1300 South State Street in Salt Lake City.

After junior high school, I went to Murray High School for one semester then to South High School for two and a half years.

At Lincoln, I was the sixth man on the basketball team. It was my first opportunity to be given a uniform and the chance to play any sport on an organized team. We lost almost every game during our first year. In my last year, we got a new coach who was a good football coach. He was only at Lincoln for two years before he transferred to West High School and had much success as their head football coach. He shaped us up for basketball and we won most of our games that second year. We even beat Irving Junior High's team once, which was the only time they'd ever been beaten that year.

The coach would drive the starting five players to the away games in his personal car. The rest of the team had to take the public city bus. On our own we played some other junior high school's baseball games. The coach lined up the games but never coached us or went to the games. Basketball was the only organized sport for junior high school competition between schools. We had lots of fun and were good in baseball also. I don't think we ever lost a baseball game.

My last year at Lincoln, I was elected Noon Hour Manager which was a student body office. There were four student body offices in junior high school. President, vice president, secretary and noon hour manager. The noon hour manager was the job for "an athlete." The job involved organizing activities and games to occupy the students during the noon hour. I mainly checked out soccer balls and softballs and bats. It wasn't a very good experience because I also had to collect and return the equipment after the lunch period. I was an equipment manager and didn't obtain any experience in student government or leadership.

Starting in 1932 and ending in 1952, the Salt Lake City School District set up a program to allow students to graduate in eleven years. Students could elect to take a 12th year. This program was only for the Salt Lake City School District. There were such critical money problems during the Great Depression that by eliminating a year of schooling a great deal of money could be saved. Most students opted to graduate after eleven years, but a lot of athletes would come back for the third year, as it was called.

The reason that I attended Murray High School was because Sam had gone there after my father bought the Murray Café in 1944 during World War II. Sam really liked going to Murray High and I thought it would be fun. It turned out to be a poor decision on my part.

Probably the biggest item a young boy wanted in those days was a bicycle. A bike opened up a new world, especially for kids whose families didn't have cars. I always wanted a new bike. Sam, being the oldest, got three new bicycles as we grew up. I was happy to get two of his hand-me-down bikes when he was finished with them. Finally, the day came when I bought a new mountain bike – I was about fifty-five years old. That event fulfilled a childhood dream to own a new bike.

During our summer vacations while school was out, we took some long bike trips with our friends to the airport or the zoo. These trips were around fifteen miles. My world was getting bigger. We also rode our bikes to the state capitol building or into town. The state capitol building had displays from each of Utah's counties, which I enjoyed. I also enjoyed the racecar called the Mormon Meteor, which had set several world speed-records for endurance at the Bonneville Salt Flats. The racecar was on display in the capital building.

Mom would pack a lunch for Sam and me and we would take our bike trips with our friends from the neighborhood. It was a real adventure as well as a fun time. Once or twice, I got very sunburned because we would take our shirts off and never wore any sun block or sun tan lotion. Those items cost money and were not used by kids.

For my eleventh birthday, mom gave me a big party and bought me an accordion. Mother always liked the accordion and that had a big influence on me. Sam took trumpet lessons and Margaret took piano lessons. I took lessons for about a year and a half. Part of the time the accordion teacher came to our house, and part of the time I took the bus to my lessons. My last teacher lived about one mile away and I would ride my bike with the accordion.

When the cold weather came and World War II started in 1941, my interest declined and I quit playing the accordion. I started taking accordion lessons again at age seventy-two and I enjoy it very much now.

For a while, Margaret took tap dancing lessons uptown. Mom would give me some money to take Margaret on the bus to her lesson. I guess I was about twelve at the time. I didn't like sitting with the mothers and watching the girls dance so I would walk around town and window-shop and then return when the lesson was over.

On December 7, 1941 when World War II started for the United States, Sam, his friend, and I were standing on the corner of State Street and Harvard Avenue. We were waiting for the bus to go to the Utah Theater to see a movie.

Some young men in a car stopped and said, "The Japs bombed Pearl Harbor."

We had never heard of Pearl Harbor. We went to the movie and the picture was interrupted several times with bulletins about early combat action. We had played soldiers and war games as little boys, but little did we know of the changes that the world would undergo because of the war and how it would affect us. Rationing of food, shoes, gas, soap, and other items were instigated. The country completely mobilized and went to war. Eventually eighteen million Americans went into the military service. The US population at that time was 120 million. No one protested about the war or any hardships caused by it. All of the young men on our street were drafted or volunteered for the military service. One of the Harvard Avenue boys that I really liked was killed early in the war. His name was Bruce Blake. He was the fellow who didn't come to the vacant house when we were locked in the cabinet.

One of only two photos of entire family taken together 1943

I have a scar on my chin where I got my first stitches when Bruce and I were racing Sam and several neighborhood boys to play hockey with a tin can and sticks. This was on a nice cement dance floor where the building had burned down. We were a block behind the group. Everyone had his roller skates on except Bruce, who had his bicycle and could go faster than the rest of us. He told me to get on the bike and ride double. After we rode a short distance, my skates got caught in the spokes of his front wheel. We both went over forward and I was knocked unconscious for a short period of time. I got the two stitches in my chin and Bruce had to replace all but two spokes on his front wheel.

Swimming was a real treat for me when I was young. No one ever had the opportunity to take swimming lessons – you just learned from the older boys.

About the time I was "learning," a group of boys that included Sam and my friends took the bus to a swimming pool called Wasatch Springs. The older boys encouraged me to jump off the diving board for the first time in my life. I couldn't swim but the older boys said they would help me if I couldn't jump far enough to reach the side of the pool. I finally mustered up all my courage and jumped. I didn't make it to the side and the older boys didn't help me. I was struggling and gasping to stay afloat and was in trouble. The lifeguard saw me and dived in to rescue me. He then used some strong words and told me to go to the shallow end of the pool and stay there. It taught me another one of life's lessons about taking chances and depending on others who might not keep their word.

Sam helped me learn to swim while I was quite young. However, I never became a strong swimmer. I enjoy swimming to this day but don't like the water to be cold.

Wars are terrible, but when the U.S.A. was involved in World War II, it was nice to have everyone united behind our leaders and military people. We were asked to collect all scrap metal for the war effort. This included tin cans and foil used to wrap items. I remember asking my father if the U.S.A. would eventually become involved in the European war, which started in 1939 – two years before the United States entered the war in 1941. He said he thought we would, and he was right.

I also remember during the summer, getting up before anyone in my family, except my dad who had gone to work, and reading the newspaper reports about the war. One frightening experience I had during the early part of the war was when a special delivery letter was delivered to our house. I didn't know anything about special delivery letters. The postman delivered the letter to my mother and she had to sign for it. The letter was from the State Department and said she was an enemy alien and needed to register immediately because we were at war with Germany. I knew about the forced evacuation of all the Japanese (citizens and non citizens) from

Gus Estimate age 9

the west coast to internment camps. I was afraid the government might do that to my mother and wondered what would happen to me. Fortunately, mother quickly went in, took the exam, and became as U.S. citizen. I assume that with mom immigrating at a young age, the family was ignorant of the fact that she wasn't a citizen.

In the wintertime, we spent our time in snowball fights, building snow forts, snowmen, sleigh riding, and those types of outdoor activities. We had lots of fun playing Monopoly and listened to the radio when indoors. Once, Mr. Short, our neighbor, crowded five or six boys into his car and drove us to the foothills to sleigh ride. We got so cold that we went inside to the zoo because our pants were freezing where they had gotten wet. I borrowed a pair of skis but never made it to the bottom without falling. I knew that someday I wanted to be a skier.

I had a very happy childhood. My first meeting and encounter with my future brother in law, Bob Forsgren, came at Liberty School. Some of us younger boys were playing basketball and we were using the one basket that didn't require anyone to look into the sun when shooting the ball. The big guys eight to ten years older, came along and told us we had to move to the basket blinded by sunlight. We said 'no' because we were there first. They threw our ball a few times to the other basket and we would come back and interfere with the big guys. Finally, one of the boys, who I think was Bob, kicked me in the seat of the pants and told us to get down to the other basket, which we did. I have never let him forget that incident and we have laughed about it many times. Kids just worked things out without involving parents in those days.

For a while I was given the nickname "Dynamite," which the older neighborhood guys had given to me. I don't know why. Every one got along very well.

There was one Jewish Family who had a boy Sam's age and a boy my age. Their names were Saul and Sidney Safran. All the other boys along the street were members of the Mormon Church. I was baptized into the Mormon Church, along with Sam, on October 2, 1938. The Block Teachers, now called the Home Teachers, came to our house. This was the only time I ever remember them coming by the house. They told mother that Sam and I should be baptized. We were taken to the Salt Lake Tabernacle and baptized. I think mom was with us, but can't remember for sure. I don't think my dad knew that we were baptized. Sam, Margaret, and myself, were all baptized into the Greek Orthodox Church as infants.

Quite often we went to ward shows, which were movies shown at the ward house building on Friday nights. This is where I saw my first movies. It was a big deal then. I remember at times Sam would carry me on his back part way home when I was tired. We must have seen our first movies when I was about five years old. Margaret was too young so Sam and I would walk to Liberty Ward, which was about a half mile away.

In 1937, Harvard Ward was built and then we went there to the ward shows. At that time, it was safe to go places in the neighborhood without fear or any harm coming your way. It was common for people to not lock their doors.

I was a Boy Scout for a year and a half and obtained the rank of Star Scout. I had ten merit badges. Eleven were needed to be a Life Scout. I lost interest because I really wanted to go to a Boy Scout Camp in the mountains or go hiking, but the Troop only went to Tracy Wigwam for one day during that entire eighteen months. I enjoyed that. I wasn't one of the "in guys" and was not able to get in the scout patrol that I wanted to belong too. I have always been sorry I did not become an Eagle Scout. I think it would have been easy had I been given some encouragement, and particularly if I'd belonged to a troop that did more outside activities.

I liked scouting and am very happy that my three sons became Eagle Scouts. When I started Lincoln Junior High School, my world got bigger, mainly by coming into contact with a great many more boys my age. Basketball was the only school sponsored sport and I loved it. I was the 6th man on the school basketball team each year. That was years before little league programs came into being. I remember going to Municipal Ball Park and being rather shy, I had a hard time to get some of the boys to play catch with me. A few of the boys' dads were there and they never showed any interest in me.

Finally, I succeeded in getting on a team and played for Ted's Glass team. I think we won the league. There were very few leagues around the city. Kids' teams had a team shirt and a hat. That was the extent of a uniform. My great love for baseball started at that time. My closest friends changed from the boys on Harvard Avenue to boys who like competitive sports. I always liked and remained friends with the neighborhood boys but we just didn't have much in common and ended up going our different directions.

The Harvard Avenue boys' names were Roy Short, Dale Radditz, Bob Mac Mellen, Gale Bateman, the Safrin Brothers, (Saul and Sid), Tom Chamberlain, and a few others who were in the neighborhood for a few years before they moved away. I really admired Russel Ingersol who was ten or twelve years older than me and lived directly across the street. He was the only adult who took me hunting a couple of times and treated me good. A few times he would rehearse for Roy Short and me some kind of a special act he had planned for a new girl he was dating. Russ was a good-looking ladies man and dated a lot. He thought up special things to impress his dates.

Harvard Avenue Boys I grew up with Sam & Gus on back row

One time Russ arranged for a blind date for his friend with his future wife's girl friend. Russ's friend ducked down in the car while he went to the door and told the two young ladies that his regular friend was unavailable but he had a substitute, which was me at about age twelve. Upon Russ's signal I got out of the car with a fancy dress hat pulled down low and a big oversized coat that hung way over my hands. I went up to the girls clapped my hands and said, "Which one is my date." The girls were much relieved when the real date got out of the car.

I wrote letters to Russ when he was in Patton's Third Army during World War II. Russ survived the war, but died from lung cancer after the war. He was 36 years old and had smoked cigarettes all his adult life.

I still remember one time when I was four or five years old, Margaret was still sleeping in a baby bed in our parent's bedroom. Sam and I slept in the second bedroom. We misbehaved big time to really upset mother and then we wouldn't go to bed when we were told to. When my dad came home, he got upset because mother was so upset. When dad said he was going to punish us, we quickly crawled under our double bed for safety. Dad took off his belt and lifted the bed up and I thought we would be killed. I don't think he touched us but we yelled and cried as if we were about to die. I never remember our dad laying a hand on anyone. It wasn't very often that mother had to discipline us.

I remember another time when we were quite small; mom grabbed the broom and wanted to whack Sam for misbehaving. He crawled around the dinning room table so fast that mom couldn't catch up to him. It ended with great laughter from mother, Sam, Margaret, and me. Dad wasn't home.

In 1937, our parents had an extra bedroom built on the back of our house. After Margaret grew too big for a baby bed and was moved out of our parents bedroom into the bedroom that Sam and I were using. Sam and I slept on a hide-a-bed couch in the front room for a couple of years. Eventually, we moved into the newly built bedroom that was nice, but didn't have any heat. We had to keep the door closed during the wintertime because it made a big part of the house cold. So Sam and I slept in the only room that didn't have any heat.

The first time I traveled out of Utah was when I was nine years of age and Uncle Nick (Dad's Brother) invited mom and us, as children to Las Vegas. We had the opportunity to meet some of my father's relatives and I enjoyed that. It was my first ride on a train. We stayed for one week. It was very exciting to see Hoover dam and ride in a boat on Lake Mead. Driving to California at the age of sixteen was the second time that I left Utah.

At about age ten, Babe Ruth came to Salt Lake City to the Community Baseball Park. The ballpark has had several names over the years. It was located four blocks from my house. He was the biggest sports figure in the world at that time. Mother was nice enough to give me money for a ticket. When I got to the ballpark, I found the regular ticket prices had been increased because this was Babe Ruth Night. I took a short cut to run home for more money and ran through a coal yard. There wasn't a fence around the yard. Suddenly a big German Shepard watchdog ran at me in a very ferocious manner. I was scared the dog would really hurt me and froze in my tracks. When the dog got to me he stopped and growled but did not bite me. I noticed he had a big chain connected to his dog collar. I waited a minute or two and then started to pet him. He was just fine except that every time I took a step away, he would growl. I had to take several slow steps before the chain was fully extended and then I made my get-away. I never took that short cut again.

I was thrilled to see Babe Ruth hit some balls over the fence. He left early because he didn't feel good. I found out later that he already had cancer, which eventually killed him.

Baseball was bigger than football, basketball, Nascar, and hockey combined at that time. There was no TV in those days.

Another time, I went to see a donkey baseball game and right after the game started a big thundershower started. I thought I should go, ran home, and got totally soaked. The ballpark stands had a roof and I could have stayed dry but I didn't think about that then. After a short time the sun came out, and I went back to the ballpark. I had to stand on the fence and watch the game. That was when I learned about rain checks. That was another lesson I learned in the 'school of hard knocks'.

Many times I went to the outside of the ballpark to try to get a foul ball, which would get you a ticket for the game. It was extremely rare that I ever got a foul ball, so I would watch the game hanging on the fence. After the seventh inning, the ticket people stopped charging for admission and you could go inside the ballpark. Good baseballs were really hard to come by, so we tried to get foul balls that were hit over the fence. Big boys were hired to retrieve the balls and would actually beat up kids who tried to run away with a foul ball.

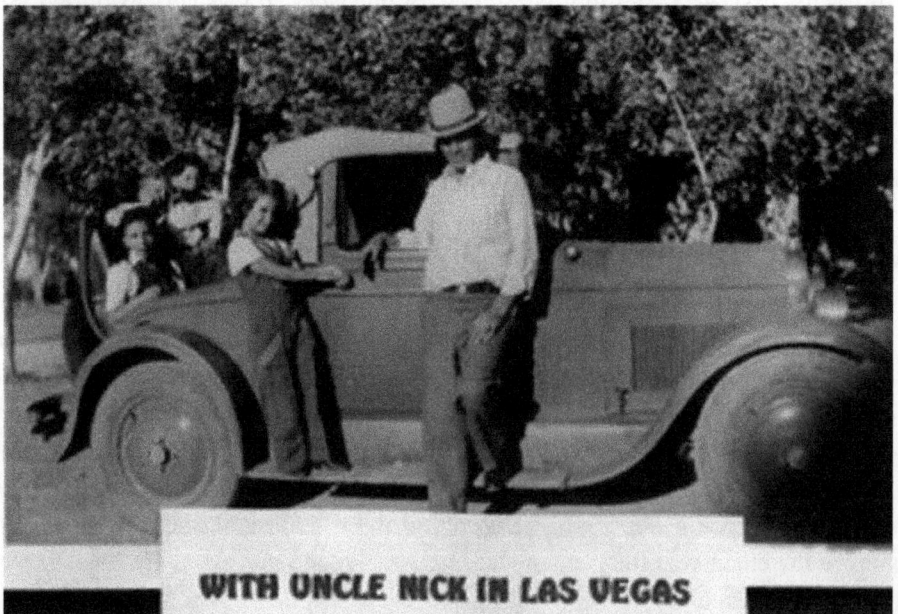

WITH UNCLE NICK IN LAS VEGAS

Sam, Margaret, Cousin Sam, and Uncle Nick 1939 and Gus

An Autobiography

We frequently played baseball with a tennis ball or anything else we could find. I loved baseball. Sometimes we would use a broomstick for a bat and rocks for the ball. Times were very different. I don't think today's children realize all the advantages they have with equipment, facilities, and organizations created just for playing sports. It is amazing to me, all the new activities kids have, including electronic gadgets, games, etc. available today that were unknown in my time. It is a historical fact throughout history that each new generation has many more advantages over the previous generation.

I saw lots of baseball games and was happy we lived close to the Salt Lake Bees baseball field. I loved everything about the game. At that time baseball was the All-American game and no other sport came close to it. It was always referred to as 'America's favorite pastime'.

Professional football and basketball were very small compared to baseball. College sports were not big like they are now. Games were broadcast only by radio. It was before the advent of TV. All of the interest, fans, and big money were put into baseball.

As kids, we dreamed of being a big league ball player or fighting in the Civil War or being a scholar.

One time, our the sixth grade class walked about one mile to sing at South High school for some event. It was the first time I had special feelings for a girl. We were walking in groups and I wanted to impress this girl. It was wintertime and snow was on the ground. Some boys were throwing snowballs at a group of girls in front of us. No one could throw far enough to reach the girls. I knew I could throw farther than the other boys and was looking for an opportunity to show off. I made a special snowball and threw it. As it neared the girls, some kids shouted out and unfortunately, the girls turned around just in time for one of them to get hit in the face. To make matters worse it was the best friend of the one I was trying to impress. The girl that got hit cried and I really felt bad – I got told off by the special girl I liked. That put a quick end to that "romance." The next day I made it a point to apologize to the girl that was hit with the snowball. She was very gracious about it.

About the time Sam turned twelve, he stood up to our mother in a little dispute. She decided it was best not to try to discipline him because he was getting so big. About a year later, I was getting ready to go to school and was acting up and giving my mother a hard time. I was out of line and deserved correction. Mother slapped me on my cheek. It didn't hurt and I laughed, mother started to cry. I really felt bad – poor mom had to handle all of the discipline problems. Fortunately, there weren't many.

Mom pretty much let Sam and I do what we wanted. She usually knew where we were and whom we were with. We never got into any serious trouble.

As a youth, my only encounter with the law came about this time when a police officer gave Sam and me a ticket for riding double on a bicycle. Mother and Margaret were waiting for a bus and were present when the officer wrote up the ticket. Mom had gone to grade school with the officer, but he still gave us the ticket.

Broken arm after car accident

Graduation Day 6/15/1957

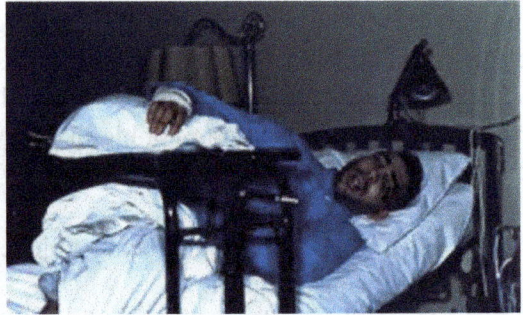

Captain A.

First VW (note cast on broken right arm)

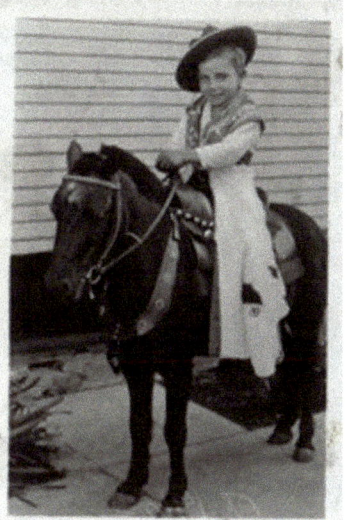

4 years on traveling pony

Gus 2 years 9 months (Didn't want
photo taken)

Scout Master Top of Mt Olympus

"Civil War Family"

Revisit Athletic Dorm

Russ McDonald's Pitts aerobic plane

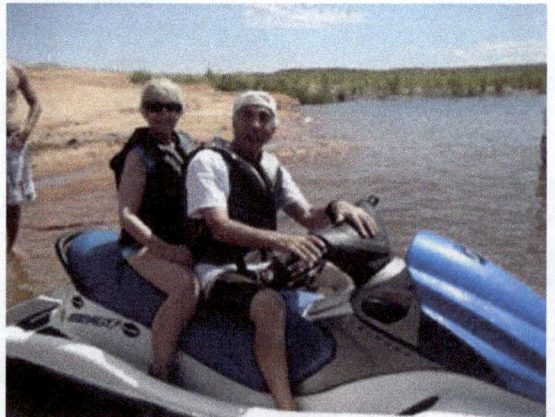

Lake Powell 2010

A few years later, Sam, and my friend Bob Sanders, and I were throwing snowballs at a street light a few houses away from our house one night after a snowstorm. The streetlights were carbon arc lights in those days. My hands got cold and I went into our house just before a police officer drove by and gave Sam and Bob a ticket. A snowball hit and broke the light just as the officer was driving on our street. Sam and Bob had to appear before the Juvenal judge with a parent. It happened to be around the time due for Sam and me to get new shoes. So during dad's afternoon break, we went to town and met dad. After we bought the shoes we went to the Police Station with dad. The judge gave a stern lecture to Bob and Sam and decided it would be good for me to hear it as well. I always thought it was funny that I just missed being caught. Dad wasn't happy about the incident. Since that time, I have had a few traffic tickets for speeding or parking but never anything else. More times than not, I have been given warning tickets for exceeding the speed limit. My children always thought I was very lucky to get the warning tickets, which didn't impose a fine.

I always wanted to spend time in the mountains as a boy. It didn't happen because my dad worked all the time and I had no uncles, grandfathers, or anyone to take me. We didn't have a car and had no Church connections. I finally came up with a plan at about age twelve or thirteen. My mom always trusted me, so during the summer, two of my friends, Dick Popkins and Bob Sanders, and I rode our bicycles up Big Cottonwood Canyon. We pulled my brother's wagon with a rope. We needed the wagon to carry our sleeping bags, food, and other supplies. We didn't know a thing about camping. We even tried to bring our dog, but he would not stay in the wagon so we left him home.

Sam & Gus about 1943

We didn't consider that coming down the canyon the rope tied to the wagon would not follow a bike the same as it would going up hill. Going down the hill the wagon at the end of a rope would start to pass the bike and be out of control, especially if the bike brakes were applied. We went to Storm Mountain in Big Cottonwood Canyon and stayed there for two nights. I caught my first fish in the reservoir there. When it was time to return home, we ran into a problem trying to "pull" the wagon downhill with a rope tied to my bike. We asked a man with a car if he would put the wagon on the back of his car and leave it at the bottom of the canyon. He agreed and we all started down the canyon. After a short distance the wagon slipped and was about to start dragging behind the car. It was my brother's good wagon and I didn't want it to get damaged. I sped up on my bike to tell the driver about the problem with the wagon. A couple of cars were coming up the canyon on the two-lane highway. I was traveling faster than the car and couldn't pass. We all came together on a bridge at the "S curve" and I put my brakes on so I would not run into any of the cars. It was a steep hill and I was going real fast. My brakes broke. I quickly put my right foot down to drag it so I would slow down. It was a very dangerous situation. My shoe came off and I didn't realize it. I continued to drag my foot and tore up the bottom of my foot. It did slow me enough to avoid the cars and to get across the bridge. I steered my bike up the mountain as soon as I got across the bridge and stopped.

Luckily, my torn up foot was the only injury, which was minor. As I couldn't continue down the canyon without out any brakes on my bike, my friends coasted down the canyon without me. The wagon stayed with me. Dick phoned his Dad who had a truck and they came to pick me up. It was a fun trip. I have told some of my grandchildren about the incident, and we all have had a good laugh.

On the same trip there were some girls about our age who were staying at a girl's camp. I tried to show off by throwing a rock at a squirrel. The rock didn't go where I aimed, but the squirrel had moved and the rock hit the squirrel and killed it. The poor squirrel happened to be in the wrong place at the wrong time. The girls got mad and told me off. I felt very bad about the squirrel. I think that was the last time I ever tried to show off to impress any girl.

My world became bigger when I left grade school. The number of students at Lincoln Junior High was about 1200. Classes were pretty easy. I didn't work very hard and got pretty good grades. I took a type class at Lincoln Junior High School. There were only two boys in all of the type classes. In those days, most girls took type so they could be secretaries. It turned out that I could type faster than anyone in my class and was one of the best in the school. The other boy in the class was the slowest typist. Knowing how to type really served me well as time went on for college papers, letters, and things like that – and now for computers.

Lincoln Junior High School. Thirteenth South and State Street –
Now a strip mall

When I started Lincoln Junior High, Sam was in his last year there. I liked being at the same school with Sam that year. I was able to play handball during the noon hour with Sam and his friends. During the first week of school, while I was eating my sack lunch, a boy who knew Sam, asked for my name. He was a popular boy and I was thrilled when he came over and gave me a big 'hello' and called me by name. He quickly asked me if I had any money. On occasion, Mom would give me a nickel for an ice cream to go with my sack lunch. I told the fellow sure and he borrowed my nickel and promised to pay me back the next day.

When I asked him for the money the next day, he said, "Kid, I don't owe you any money. I don't even know who you are."

That nickel was a great investment in learning about some people's character and their lack of integrity.

High School Years

I couldn't wait to start high school so I could participate in sports. I played on the sophomore football team at Murray High. We didn't have any games. I did okay and enjoyed it. I was cut off the Murray High School basketball team and transferred to South High for spring semester. I went out for baseball and was on the varsity baseball team as a possible starter, but was ruled ineligible because of my transfer from a different school.

State Champs 1946

Jimmy Gilbert was the baseball coach and was the best baseball coach in the state. The following year I played football and was first string on the junior varsity team. I was also second string of the varsity football team. I tried out for basketball but didn't make the team. When spring came around, the Coach asked me to play in the outfield because Dick Taylor played third base and couldn't run very well due to an accident. A large bus had run over him and broken his pelvis. Up to that point I usually played third base. I was happy to be first string.

They'll Be Swingin' Today

That was a great year. We lost the first game 2-1 to Ogden High School and then won all of the rest of the games to win the state championship. By then Bob Sanders, Dick Walkingshaw, Dick Taylor, and Wayne Swenson were my closest friends. Sanders struck out in the championship game against Bingham. I wound up being the top hitter on the team with a .454 batting average. That was a great team.

An Autobiography

Eventually, seven players from that high school team played professional baseball in the minor leagues. I don't think any high school baseball team turned out that many professional players from one team in the history of the State of Utah. As a matter of fact, all seven players went to the same Junior High School. The only high school sports game of any kind that my parents saw me play was the game we won for the state baseball championship in 1946. They did see the High School All Star Baseball game I played in shortly after graduation.

Mom and Dad also saw a couple of my professional baseball games. They never saw any of my basketball or football games, though. Very few parents ever attended high school games in those days.

I loved football and did pretty well in high school. As mentioned earlier, during my first year at South High, I was first string on the junior varsity team and second string on the varsity. I remember the first varsity game I suited up for was an 'away' game. While the team was getting dressed, some fellows said the coach was

Coach Ryan and some key returning letterman

hollering my name and wanted to see me. I was excited and couldn't imagine why the coach would want me before an important game. It turned out that one of the main varsity players forgot his shoulder pads and the coach wanted him to use mine.   That year, I got to play in a few varsity games after the game had been decided. One game against Ogden High School, the first string player in front of me had been injured in the previous game, so I started and played the whole game. That was really fun. I had a good game and was able to recover two fumbles. I think we lost that game, however. We didn't win too many games that year.

Gus G. Angelos

I went back to high school for a third year, was co-captain of the varsity football team, and played both offense and defense. That was the first year the rules for football were changed so that teams could have unlimited substitution. The coach, Pat Ryan, had me play three different offensive and three different defensive positions that year. It was really fun. We started out very strong, but had injuries to a couple of key players so we didn't win a lot of games that year. Looking back, our coach was a nice man, but not a very good football coach. We had a lot of talent and could have been a good team if we had had a good coach.

As for basketball my senior year, I tried out again and didn't make the team. My friends and I played on an Elks Boy's Club basketball team. We played a practice game against South High's Junior Varsity team and beat them by about twenty points. We played the varsity, and they only beat us by three. We played a lot of games and had a good team. I like basketball and played on many LDS church teams until I was about forty-five years old.

Prep Stars Await Diamond Tilt

Clean up hitter for South All Star Team

Come the spring of 1947, we had had a good baseball year, but had lost in the playoffs. We could have easily won the state again had all the eligible players come back for their third year. Walkingshaw and Sanders both went professional and did very well, pitching in the minor leagues.

An Autobiography

I have a big scrapbook of my baseball days. My senior year, I led the baseball team in hitting again with a batting average around .400. I was the captain. I was honored to be chosen the 'Outstanding Baseball Player' of the school. I made the all-state team. In the State All Star baseball game, I was the number-four hitter with two triples. I came in third place for a trip to Chicago to play in an All American All-Star game. One player from Utah got to go to Chicago. I was disappointed I wasn't selected but knew by then that life has its ups and downs.

That summer, I went to a Dodger tryout camp and they offered a contract to me to play professional baseball. I was also invited to a St. Louis Cardinal Baseball Camp because a baseball scout had seen the All-Star game. I had a scholarship offer from the football coach, Dick Romney, to play football at Utah State. The other co-captain of the football team at South High School was named Harold Romney. His uncle Dick Romney was the head football coach at Utah State. I was not sure what this invitation or scholarship involved but I think it was because I was a pretty good high school football player.

Still, baseball was my first love and I was better at baseball. We had the best high school baseball coach in the state. His name was Jimmy Gilbert. His high school teams won several state baseball championships. I was greatly honored years later when he retired that he had chosen me as one of the players on his All Star Team – out of all of the players he had coached during his career.

Gilbert had a wonderful way with boys and was a great role model for all of us. Twenty years later, Gilbert started me playing tennis on a regular basis. We also skied several times together. It was a wonderful experience to become good friends as adults. We reminisced a lot about people, places, and life. Gilbert had a very positive influence on me and many, many young men. He had a great sense of humor and never put anyone down.

When I graduated from high school, I weighed about 170 pounds and was about 5 feet 11 inches tall at seventeen years old. I loved high school and never had any trouble with any of the easy classes that I took. My second and third year, I had a lot of fun in the acappella choir. The Music Teacher was named Armont Willardson, who died in June 2003 at the age of 92. He was the last of my high school teachers to pass away.

South High School 1947 - Now the building is the South Campus of Salt Lake Community College

When I tried out for the choir, I thought most athletes had bass voices. I don't know where I ever got an idea like that. I knew I couldn't sing low notes, so I just went with the baritones, as Mr. Willardson didn't tell me where to go. During one early morning rehearsal I was told that I was a tenor and that the choir needed tenors. I told the teacher I would rather not move, but he insisted, and I went with the second tenors.

A couple of months later during another early morning rehearsal, I was informed I was a first tenor and the choir needed first tenors more than any other group. I was offered the number two seat, although it didn't mean anything to me to be in the number two seat. The choir director rated singers and put them in seats accordingly for the first half of each section. I didn't think I had a very good voice, but it was his call. I still didn't want to move but was told I had to, so I did. It was a very good high school choir and had over 200 members. The number one tenor was a boy named Richard Storrs and singing was his passion. Even though I didn't know anything about vocal music, I thought he had a shallow voice and was an average singer. He was short and very slender, but he loved singing and was a nice guy. It was a great learning experience for me to meet him years later in Germany where he had been studying voice for ten years. He had a marvelous voice and was the lead tenor at the Pfortzheim Opera Company in Germany.

Richard returned to the U.S. and was a soloist for the Mormon Tabernacle Choir. By that time he had gained about 50 pounds and had an outstanding voice. He was a soloist for some of the early recordings of the choir.

I didn't go to many of the high school singing performances with the choir and was consequently moved out of the number two seat, which didn't bother me. When I look back with hindsight, I wished I had participated more. Mr. Willardson even asked me to try out for the lead tenor part in an operetta, but again I was immature and not interested. I did have the ability to sing on pitch and learn quickly. I don't think the quality of my voice was very good. Maybe average at best. Hay fever affected my speaking voice and my singing voice. People still at times ask me if I have a cold because of the nasal tone of my voice.

My grades in high school were okay. Many years later, I found out that I had graduated in the upper third of my class of 825 students. That was a big surprise to me. I could have done better in school and could have been active in more student activities, but I was immature and should have had a better attitude. None of my close friends were interested in getting good grades or participating in any activities other than sports. I took the lazy way out and took easy subjects with my peer group. We were good athletes and didn't get into smoking or drinking or doing any bad things. Drugs were unknown in those days. None of my friends went to church except Wayne Swenson.

At South, a couple of acquaintances asked me to run for a student body office, but I refused. I was quite popular because of sports. I elected to take really easy classes in order to be with my friends, and was not interested in going to college. I was immature and short sighted about the value of an education. Of my closest friends, only Wayne Swenson and Dick Taylor went to college. Taylor didn't graduate. There were so many seminary classes at South High that no one knew who was a Mormon or who wasn't. About one quarter of the students in high school went on to college in those days. I wanted to take an auto mechanics class like Sanders and Walkingshaw, but the Dean of Boys would not approve it. I am thankful for that decision now. That was a three-hour class and an opportunity to really goof off.

I talked some of my friends into taking physics class because one science class was required for graduation. They all checked out after the first day when they found out it might be a hard class. I was interested in physics, but I succumbed to peer pressure and dropped the class.

On that first day of the physics class, the teacher told us what we would be studying. He asked a question about the metric system. I was the only one who knew the answer. My friends kidded me about being "a brain." I don't know where I had learned anything about the metric system.

A few years later, I paid dearly for not having taken college prep classes. At the University of Wyoming, I was the only one in all of my science classes that did not have any high school background in physics, chemistry, or advanced math. I will write more about that later. High School years were a very carefree time.

World War II ended while I was in high school. The U.S.A. emerged as the most powerful country and by far the richest. Europe and Asia were in ruins. My outlook at that time was, 'why go to college?' I thought the custodians made as much money as the teachers did, and they didn't waste four years in college.

Jobs were plentiful and unskilled heavy labor jobs paid well. I remember standing in line at my high school graduation and thinking I would never take another test in my life. That was a happy thought. Little did I realize that I would go to college for eight years plus three additional years of specialty training. All my close friends were one or two years older than me and got interested in girls earlier than I did. I never dated until I was sixteen years old. During my last year in high school, I started to date and had my first girlfriend named Barbara Nelson. She pursued me. I though it was because I was popular because of sports. Barbara wanted to break up shortly after I graduated, and it was for the best.

I met Pearl at the end of my second year when her family came to see Joy, Pearl's older sister, graduate. One of my friends had taken Joy to the Award Dinner Dance. I went to the graduation to see many of my friends graduate, and there I was introduced to Pearl and her family. I thought she was cute. During my last year in high school, Pearl went to all the games. We were friendly but never dated. It was good for me to attend my last year of high school after my close friends had graduated. It gave me a whole new outlook and perspective on life, even though I was envious of Sanders and Walkingshaw playing professional baseball.

One time, my girlfriend Barbara asked me what I wanted to do for a career when I graduated. I told her I wasn't sure if I wanted to play professional football or professional baseball. What an immature dreamer. Two times during my teen years, my father told me I should cut back on sports and get a job and save money so that I could go to college. I told my Dad I really liked sports, and he let it go without any further discussion. That is the only time I remember that my dad gave me some advice about education or the future.

Most every boy at one time or another wanted to be a pilot and that was a dream I had at a very young age. My brother wanted to be a train engineer.

Gus G. Angelos

Jobs

Throughout my growing up years, money was hard to come by. I never had an allowance. The first money I ever earned was earned by going to the grocery store for a crippled widow lady who lived across the street from us. She would give me a list of items to buy and then reward me with a nickel. I also tried to sell *Liberty* magazine subscriptions and found out I was not a good salesman. I did knock on doors and got a few jobs mowing lawns. That was before the days of power lawn mowers. The job consisted of cutting the front and back yard grass, raking it, and trimming the edges of the lawn by hand and cleaning up. The price was twenty-cents. I remember a time or two when I would earn a quarter, ride the bus for a nickel to town, go to a movie for ten cents, buy a candy bar for a nickel and then go home. I did this all by myself. The admission price to a movie was ten cents if you were under twelve years of age.

My first indoor job at age thirteen was at Johnson's Ice Cream Store, which was two blocks from my house. Wayne Swenson was working there and when the boss, Dan Johnson, asked Wayne if he had any friends that wanted a job, Wayne suggested me. Dan told Wayne he didn't want a Greek working there, so I wasn't hired until one time when they got desperate. I was hired as the dishwasher for thirty-five cents an hour. After a short while, I moved up to scooping ice cream and making malts and stuff like that. Dan liked me and asked Wayne if he knew of 'any other good workers like Gus'."

Sam also worked there for a while. It was a fun job and very busy in the summer time when the War was on. Sugar was rationed and ice cream was a real treat during that time because everyone had an icebox. Ice cream melted in an icebox.

Gus G. Angelos

On a few occasions, we would play tennis with the boss. One Saturday while playing tennis, I borrowed a quarter from the boss. I never did anything like that and don't remember why. On Monday, I was ill and sent a quarter with Swenson to give to the boss. The boss thought that was funny and kidded me if I was afraid I was going to die and still owe him a quarter. I learned from my parents to pay your debts and live within your means. Years later I realized what an incident like that can tell an employer about the character of a thirteen year old.

One summer during the War, Sam, I, and some of our friends worked at a cannery in Murray canning peas. We worked from six in the evening till six in the morning. I think I only lasted half the summer. A couple of years later when I was fifteen, I applied for a summer job at Utah Fire Clay doing heavy unskilled labor. Sanders and Walkingshaw worked there too. Employees were supposed to be sixteen but no one checked to see if I was underage.

I even had to join the Teamster Union. It was a hard, hot job, making brick and pipe. I would personally handle 15,000 bricks twice a week. The pay was seventy-five cents an hour. You could support a family on that amount of money.

Wages were frozen during the War. I eventually worked for about five summers at the brickyard.

Cars

My family bought their first car, which was a 1937 Hudson car, when I was fifteen and a half years old. We all went to look at the car during dad's break. Sam was in the Merchant Marines the time. When the mechanic (salesman) asked if anyone wanted to drive the car, my mom was bashful and my dad didn't drive, so I spoke up and was allowed to drive around town for a short ride. I really didn't know much about driving, but wasn't about to pass up the chance. I killed the engine in the middle of town, but started it up again and had a great time. That was before automatic transmissions had been invented.

When I was sixteen, I bought my first car, which was a 1933 Ford Sedan. I paid $250.00 and I think insurance was about $35.00 a year – maybe it was for six months. I eventually traded that car for a yellow 1932 Ford Roadster with a rumble seat. I had the roadster my senior year in high school and really had lots of fun with it. Not many kids had cars in high school. That car was really cold in the winter. The heaters in those old cars put out very little heat. I eventually sold that car for $350.00. I always wanted to get another car like it, but now that model is a collector's item and expensive. It wouldn't be practical now, but would still be a fun toy.

In those days, if we owned a car, we worked and paid all the expenses. I never knew anyone whose parents bought a car for his or her son. Girls hardly ever drove, let alone owned a car.

In the summer of 1946, just prior to my last year in high school, my friends and I overhauled the engine of the '33 Ford Sedan. The day after we finished, Alan Wright, Dick Popkins, and myself took off for Los

Angeles. We drove the whole distance at 35 miles per hour to break in the engine. That was the way it was done in those days. What a long drive.

When we got to L. A., Dick had an aunt he wanted to stay with for a few days. We gave most of our money to Dick for safekeeping. Allen and I planned to sleep in the car but were afraid something might happen and we would lose our money.

On the first day, we went to the beach to see the Pacific Ocean for the first time. We were very tired from the long drive to California and fell asleep at the beach and got really badly sunburned.

We had a lot of car trouble driving to California and decided to have a mechanic fix it. The mechanic kept the car over night so Alan and I went to an all night movie. It was a very uncomfortable night with our sunburns and we saw the same movie over and over.

The next day, after we picked up the car, we could not find where Dick's aunt lived. When we dropped Dick off, I knew we were in a big unfamiliar city and told Alan we should write down the address. We didn't have a pencil and Alan said he knew the area because he had lived in Long Beach for one year. Much to our dismay, Alan couldn't find the place. We drove through some scary parts of the city. I had never seen anything like that before in my upbringing in Salt Lake. That was before television and unless you looked at pictures in books or had the interest to research things, you were unaware of ghettos and slums. Young people were too self-centered to think of those things. On top of that, I was sixteen and had only been out of Utah for one week out of my entire life.

In those days, movies, magazine and information had strict censorship and pornography didn't exist for young people. I didn't realize it at the time, but I was very naïve. I found out just how naïve while seventeen years old and playing baseball with men six to fifteen years older than me.

We sent a telegram to my mother to phone Dick's mom to find the address of Dick's Aunt. My Mom was then supposed to send us a telegram with Dick's address to general delivery in L. A. Well, my mom, bless her heart, took two days to respond. Alan and I ran out of money and were very low on gas. We could only afford one bowl of soup for two days. We ate all the crackers that were on the counter of the restaurant. The manager came and took away some other crackers before we could eat them. It never occurred to us to inquire if a church or county agency could feed us or that we could make a collect phone call. We were too bashful to ask anyone for food or money. It turned out to be a very good learning experience and a chance to know real hunger.

The mechanics in California didn't solve the motor problems and we had car problems on the way back to Salt Lake. We knew enough to improvise and keep the car running enough to get home. Even so, it was a fun adventurous trip.

Gus G. Angelos

Professional Baseball and on to the University of Wyoming

Signs Cardinal Contract

Gus Angeles, star outfielder of the South high baseball team of the Utah Scholastic league during the 1947 season, is now a member of the St. Louis Cardinals organization. He held down right field for Pocatello Tuesday night against Ogden Reds.

Reds, Cardinals Wind Up Current Series at Affleck Park This Evening

Ogden Reds and Pocatello Cardinals will wind up the current series at Affleck park this evening. The Reds moved ahead in the series with a colorful ninth inning triumph Tuesday to nose out the last place holders, 3 to 2.

53

Gus G. Angelos

U pon graduation from South High School in 1947, I was fortunate to have some choices that allowed me to pursue athletics. I thought seriously about attending Utah State University to play football. As I wrote earlier, I was not sure what college would be like or what the scholarship involved. I probably would have gone to Utah State University and tried to play football and baseball if I hadn't received offers to play professional baseball.

As it turned out, I grabbed the best offer – chosen between the Dodgers and Cardinals – to play professional baseball and signed a contract for $150.00 a month. I joined the Pocatello Cardinals in Pocatello, Idaho in August 1947. My parents had to sign the contract because of my age.

I always liked the St Louis Cardinals better than the Dodgers anyway. So I was very happy. Now, with good old hindsight, I wish I would have gone to college first and then gone into professional baseball.

I played my first professional baseball game when I was seventeen years and nine months of age. My first time up to bat – I struck out. My first game I went 0 hits for 3 times at bat. I was scared and inexperienced in that type of competition.

My first hit came the next night, the first time at bat. I finished the year as a substitute outfielder and pinch hitter. My batting average was in the low 200's. I was living on cloud nine and getting paid for doing something I dearly loved. All of the players on the team were World War II veterans and their ages ranged from twenty-four to thirty-six years. They all treated me good and helped me. It was quite an experience to associate and live on the road trips with these older men who had seen the world and experienced things way beyond me. I realized I had lived a very sheltered life growing up in Salt Lake.

From age twelve until seventeen, all of the older boys that I knew were away in the military service. I didn't have those older guys to look up to as roll models.

The ball club traveled in an old war surplus bus. The ball club paid for hotel rooms on the road and gave us $3.50 a day for meal money. The $3.50 was enough to buy 3 meals, nothing fancy. When we were in Pocatello (one half of each month), we paid our own room and board. I was very fortunate and was invited to stay with my Uncle Bill and Aunt Annie Angelos and their Family who lived in Pocatello. They had a small

54

neighborhood grocery store next to their house. They worked hard and long hours. Uncle Bill was my favorite Uncle. I think Uncle Bill and my Dad were second Cousins. They were very good to me and it saved me money.

During the winter of 1947-48, I phoned Pearl Trauffer on Wayne Swenson's urging and asked her to go on a double date. Wayne was going with Pearl's older sister Joy. Eventually they got engaged, but never married. We hit it off good and when I left for spring training in Fullerton California, she was my girlfriend and started writing me letters. I went to Fullerton, California in April 1948 where three of the Cardinal teams were having their spring training. There were about 200 men at spring training.

Pearl during dating years

After about three weeks, each team selected their players and I was thrilled to make the Pocatello team. They held races and I was one of the top ten men for speed. I thought I was all set. However, when we arrived at Pocatello, there were about six players who had been at spring training with higher farm teams. Unfortunately for me, two of them were outfielders. It was common in those days to move down players after spring training to lower teams. It starts with the parent team, St. Louis looking over the younger players to see what players might help them in the future.

The first two games at home, I hit two balls off the fence and I thought I had my first professional home run, but both were doubles. Again, I was used sparingly because the other three outfielders were much older and were much more experienced.

In 1947 Pocatello came in last place in the Pioneer League. In 1948 the team won the league. In the middle of the 1948 season, I asked to be sent to another team where I could play every day. The manager from the year before, Jim Tyack was managing at Willows, California. He liked me and had told me he would have me in the line up every day if I went to his team from spring training. So, I went to Willows California via Greyhound bus and upon arriving there found out that Jim Tyack had been fired a few days earlier.

A regular player was the interim manager, didn't know me, and never gave me a chance to play except for one game. I felt strongly that I could have done well, but the team was deep in last place and in financial trouble. The new manager didn't have any experience as a manager, hadn't been to spring training, and didn't know me so I was released.

I don't remember how it came about but a senior baseball scout drove me to Los Angeles to work out with the Hollywood Stars baseball team. Hollywood was an independent Triple-A team in the old Pacific Coast League. The team paid my expenses and I worked out for a week with them. That was a good experience to work out with Triple-A players. Hollywood gave me a contract to join Billings, Montana in August when they came to Salt Lake. In the mean time I went back to Salt Lake and started playing for Penny Beverage in the Utah State Industrial League. I did very well with them. Six weeks later when Billings came to Salt Lake, the manager hadn't been notified that I was to join the team, and so that deal fell through. They offered me a contract to go to spring training the following year. I finished the season with Penny Beverage.

Come 1949, I decided to go as a free agent to spring training with Tulsa Oilers to Alexandria, Louisiana, which was a Double-A team. I went with Bob Sanders, who was under contract to that team. I thought Cincinnati was a good baseball organization. I didn't make the Tulsa team but was invited to Tyler, Texas to join an independent team and so I spent a couple of weeks in Tyler, Texas. I think that might have been a good place to play except that I made a choice to go to California and join the Ogden Reds of the Pioneer League.

The Ogden team contacted me and asked me to come, and I liked the idea of playing closer to home. With Ogden I did well at spring training and led the team in hitting. Again, I thought I was all set, but when we got to Ogden, I had a very sympathetic general manager tell me I didn't fit in with their plans. The other outfielders had money invested in them. I felt bad because I had a higher batting average than anyone on the team during all the spring training games. I was released again.

The winter of 48-49 Sam and I worked for my dad as waiters in the G. & G. Lunch restaurant located at about 25 East 900 South. The G & G stood for George and George because my dad dad's last restaurant had a partner named George, who lasted for a year. There

Dad's last restaurant

were four booths and about twelve stools at the counter. The building was a small wood structure and has since been torn down. My dad had sold the Murray restaurant because it was too difficult to keep open sixteen hours a day and ride the bus to work. It took a toll on his health. I think he had the Murray Cafe for about five years and did well financially.

The G & G cafe closed on Sundays and was open about twelve hours each day. One Sunday when we were cleaning the cafe, Sam and I did something that upset my dad. I think he thought we had a poor attitude and were goofing off.

At any rate, he said something like, "Why do you think I have worked so hard all these years and about killed myself, if it wasn't for you kids?"

That remark really hurt and caused me to do some deep thinking. What dad said was true. That was the only time he ever said anything like that. He provided for us very well at a great cost, especially to his health. He had very little time for himself or for any hobbies or fun activities.

After being released from Ogden in 1949 I had a fun summer. I played baseball for Helper, Utah. We won the State Semi Pro Championship and qualified to go to Wichita, Kansas for the National Semi Pro Championships. I was paid $12.50 per game that year – in today's figures that would be about $100.00 per game. Helper paid more money to the players than any other team in the state. As luck would have it, Helper strengthened the team by picking up a few of the best players from the other teams in the league for the National Semi-Pro Tournament in Kansas. The outfielder they picked up was also a pitcher that had played in the Major Leagues. I could see I would probably be sitting on the bench. I decided not to go to Kansas.

Helper Baseball Team---Gus standing top left

Later, with 20/20 hindsight, I wished I had gone. I think my batting average was around .290 that year. It would be the last time and one of the few times my batting average was ever below .300.

College

O ne of the biggest and most important decisions I have ever made occurred at this time. It totally changed my life.

Two of the players for Helper were athletes from the University of Wyoming. The baseball coach had told them that if they discovered any good, young players that summer, to let him know. They had written the baseball coach and told him about me. I didn't know about the letter they wrote. Out of the clear blue sky I received a letter offering me an athletic scholarship to Wyoming. School was to start in three weeks. I had just sold my 1932 yellow Ford roadster and bought my first nice car, which was a two year old 1947 Chevrolet convertible. Part of the purchase included me taking over a $35.00 monthly payment for ten months. This was the first time I had ever gone into debt for anything, but felt I could easily handle the payments by continuing to work.

Three years earlier, I had loaned my Brother $350.00 so he could buy a nice car. Sam got married in the mean time and I thought he needed the money more than me, so I let the matter go. I had never thought seriously about going to college for an education, only sports. I didn't realize the value of a college education. I had never known anyone in my neighborhood that had a college education. The two seasons I played professionally really opened my eyes. I saw that most of the men would not be successful as big major league baseball players and were poorly prepared to have good careers in the work force. Security was always a big thing to me.

I was too proud to ask my parents for money to pay off the car or help me in college. I really didn't want to sell my new car so I decided to ask Sam if he would take over the payments to pay me the money he owed. He was very willing to do that as he didn't have any children and both he and his wife, Joy were working. Honestly, I don't know what I would have done had Sam not agreed to take over the payments.

Freshman photo 1949

I might add at that time, the NCAA had a rule that if you had been a professional athlete, you were not eligible to participate in any college athletics. My two friends had written the coach not knowing that I had played professionally. I talked to them they advised me that freshman could not play on varsity teams. They said I would probably get two years of free schooling in before my eligibility would be questioned. They also said they would not tell anyone and they never did.

So in September, 1949, at the age of nineteen, I started on an unknown adventure and headed east in Laramie, Wyoming. It was a very quick decision. I had never been to Wyoming. The distance to the University was exactly 425 miles from my home in SLC. I was very concerned whether I had the intellect to pass college classes, especially since I'd been out of high school for two years. The first thing I had to do was to take entrance exams, which lasted for two days. Then I met with an advisor to select classes. He helped me and I quickly decided I wanted to be a coach. That meant getting a bachelor degree in the college of education. I was told that I would have better job opportunities if I would major in science. Plus, I would be able to teach other subjects besides physical education and coach sports.

I met with the baseball coach whose main job was the top assistant football coach. My scholarship was for out of state tuition only. That amounted to $336.00 per year. I was told that if I turned out to be a good baseball player, I would get a full scholarship the following year, which would include room, board, and tuition. The coach encouraged me to go out for football, which could increase the scholarship to include meals the first year. I went out for football and found out that the players were bigger, stronger, and faster than they were in high school.

The university had lots of money, as it got royalties on all the minerals produced in the state, mainly coal, oil, and natural gas. Wyoming is still one of the leading mineral producers in the U.S.A. The U. of Wyo. was the only university in the state. It was said, they were only behind the University of California and the University of Texas with regards to income for a State University.

Wyoming had launched a gigantic building program after World Ward II, which included all new athletic complexes and facilities. New coaches were hired and the number of athletic scholarships was increased. I got the end of the line football equipment and started practicing. A l l the other football players had been practicing for two months. I hadn't played football for two years and was behind them in conditioning, as well as being familiar with the football plays on offense and defense. For some reason the coach allowed me a very brief tryout at defensive end in a scrimmage against the varsity football team. I had been out for football for about three weeks when the coach called me in and told me they like their ends to be bigger. I honestly think to this day I could have lettered on the varsity football team as a defensive halfback or as a wide receiver.

Wyoming's football team didn't pass the ball much in those days. I played mostly half back in high school and my size was okay for those positions in college. The coach offered me a job to work at the Pi Beta Phi Sorority House, which would provide two meals every day and $10.00 a month. I accepted the job so I could be self-sufficient.

Another reason for not playing football was that I knew if I played on the varsity football team I would have a picture in the football program, and people in Salt Lake would see it and probably report me for having been a professional ball player. I was totally on my own, and I didn't have enough money saved to see me through the whole school year. There weren't any student loans or grants to help me, and my parents were not in a position to help financially either. I know my parents would have found a way to help financially, but I didn't want to ask them.

For the remainder of my first year, I got by on two meals a day – lunch and dinner. The cafeteria was expensive and I could not afford to buy food at the store and keep it in my dormitory room. Laramie was also a small town (12,000 population) and part time jobs were difficult to find for college students. I wasn't sure how long I would last in college. It turned out to be a good job for my freshman year.

I went from the lowest of six guys who worked at the sorority, to the top guy at the end of the year. The black cook, Daphne really liked me, and we got along great. The meals were very good. Daphne didn't care much for the sorority girls, and she would save me special left over foods. The following year, she and her husband, Willie started cooking in the athletic dorm. Willie loved baseball the best of any of the college sports. He went to most of the games.

University of Wyoming Publicity Department – photo (never used) 1953

A short time after my football try out, the school had fall baseball tryouts open to anyone. Before the first week was over, the coach told me I had the full scholarship starting the next year. The baseball scholarship quota was full for that year. The coach even got me an additional pay job in the spring, helping the grounds keepers who worked on the baseball field. I finished my first year with a B minus average.

Baseball wasn't much for freshman. I led the freshman team in most everything. We only had a few practice games. The coach kept telling me that the NCAA was thinking about making freshman eligible to play on varsity teams. He said if they did, I would be a starter. That year the varsity team was good and really needed a right-handed hitter. I could have been a big help, but it didn't happen. The NCAA did change the rule to make freshman eligible for varsity sports, but it came two years too late for me.

That summer, a friend and I went to Iowa to play baseball. I went to Autobahn, Iowa and my friend, Chuck Afferbach went to Schaler, Iowa. We didn't make it through that season. The Korean War broke out and we came home early. I don't remember where I played the rest of the summer.

Going back to college was much easier the second year because I had an athletic scholarship that provided room and board to me. I also had friends and was familiar with the campus and college life. The athletic department had acquired a new dormitory building that held all 120 scholarship athletes. During the '50's, the University of Wyoming probably had one of the largest athletic budgets in the Skyline Conference. The Skyline Conference changed and became the Western Athletic Conference. The WAC changed and is presently the Mountain West Conference. During my four years at the University, Wyoming was the powerhouse of the conference winning titles in most every sport. The football team was seldom beaten and had an undefeated season and won the Gator Bowl my second year.

Basketball and football were either first or second in the conference all four years I was there. As to baseball, we had good teams each year, but never finished first. My senior year we were first in our division but lost the last two games to New Mexico then wound up finishing second to them by one half game. As to my individual performance, I led the team in most every offensive department for all four years. I ended up with a lifetime batting average in college of .400 even.

My last year, I hit ten home runs. One game I hit three consecutive home runs. I was told that was a school record. I have a scrapbook that Pearl keeps for me that outlines many of the things I did.

I was the captain of the baseball team my last two years. The altitude of 7,000 feet and the wind blowing all the time really made the ball go a long distance. The weather was often very cold for baseball.

Gus G. Angelos

1952 University of Wyoming Baseball Gus 2nd from left standing

One funny incident occurred that I still remember. As I started my first year on the varsity team, a veteran player from the previous year told some of the other players I wasn't very good and he would have a higher batting average than me. When the year was over my batting average was about .150 points higher than his. That year was the lowest batting average I had in college. It was .391. The following year I hit .412 and my last year I hit .397.

One game played against Denver University, I was ill and felt lousy. I didn't tell the coach because I wanted to play. That game I hit four hard line-drives in my four trips to the plate. Two went for doubles and the other two were caught by the outfielders.

One of the opposing players, who was a Greek boy, told me after the game, "I hate to see you come to bat because I know you are the best hitter and usually hit the ball hard and can hurt us."

Another time the coach, Bud Daniels gave the bunt signal, which I didn't see. There were two base runners and no outs. It wasn't a bunt situation at that point in the game. The coach was a nice guy, but didn't know the game well enough to be an outstanding coach. He did become a good coach and coached for twenty years at the university. Often he

64

would flash the signals late when coaching. At any rate, it wasn't a good call with the clean up hitter at bat early in the game. I hit a home run and the coach told me it was a good thing because I missed the signal and would have been in the doghouse.

It was absolutely great playing college baseball, hitting clean up every year, and being the star player. I played center field most of the time. I played catch a few times when we needed to pinch hit for the catcher late in the game. They are wonderful memories.

During one game against the University of Colorado, I hit a double off the wall the first time at bat. The second time at bat, I hit a home run over the right center field fence. The third time, I hit a sharp line drive single. The next two times when I came to bat during that game, I was intentionally walked. The last time at bat and no runners on base, I flied out. That was one of the best hitting days I had ever had as a player.

A scout from Cleveland was at the game and talked to me about playing professional baseball. I told him I sure would like to do that. He told me he would be in touch at the end of the season, and he kept his word. At that time, I was in good physical shape. I was 5 feet 11¾ inches tall, weighed 187 pounds, and ran sixty yards across the outfield in 6.8 seconds. I always wanted to be six feet tall or even taller, like my brother Sam. Alas, I never made it.

I had a strong throwing arm. I worked hard and still had dreams of becoming a big league baseball player.

I remember another humorous thing that happened during my senior year. I had a good friend who played for the University of New Mexico's baseball team. He was a good player and got a nice bonus to sign a professional baseball contract. He told me that before one series between the two universities, the New Mexico coach was talking to the team and they were discussing our team. My name came up as the most dangerous hitter, and the coach was talking to their best pitcher about how to pitch to me.

The pitcher told him. "If I throw him a fast ball, he hits it. If I throw him a curve, he hits it. If I throw him a change up, he hits that too. What should I do, Throw my glove up there?"

A good sense of humor is a wonderful thing.

My greatest thrill in college baseball was to hit three consecutive home runs against Ft. Warren. They had a strong pitching staff. All of them had played professional baseball in the minor leagues. I think the three consecutive home runs is still a record.

Another thing I was proud of was the fact that I never missed an inning of any game throughout high school or college. I never was injured, got into any trouble, and was valuable enough to the team to always be in the line up. Each spring, the team would go to Albuquerque, New Mexico for two weeks of spring training. The team would stay at Kirtland Air Force Base, which made it very inexpensive for rooms and meals for the school. The weather was wonderful compared to Laramie. We would open our conference games with the University of New Mexico. We would also play several practice games.

We played the professional team one year and several games against the Air Force Base Team. They had several professional players on the team during the Korean War. I bumped into a good high school teammate and friend, Clair Bailey. He managed the Air Base team, played center field, and hit clean up for them. The last year we were there, Clair got a home run, which won the first game. The next day I got a home run, which won that game. Everyone wondered why we were such good friends.

Our friendship went back to junior high school. Clair and I played together in high school. He played professional baseball but made a career of the Air Force, where he had special duty because he was such a good basketball and baseball player. Unfortunately Clair had a heart attack and died in his late forties. To date, three fellows from our high school championship team have died. When you win a state championship, a strong bond is formed. We have gotten together four or five times since 1946.

During the two summers while still in college, I played baseball at Worland, Wyoming for the Worland Indians. It was a very good semi-pro team, and they paid me well and played lots of games. I also worked a job at a lumberyard for two summers. Another summer, I worked for the local gas company. I really needed the money. I would have liked to have been in Salt Lake during those summers, though.

While at Worland, I hit clean up, played center field, and led the team each year in hitting. My batting average was usually around .350.

The team played in two leagues, plus extra games against Air Base and some traveling teams. Playing there meant I would play in many more games that I would have played in Salt Lake. Plus the money difference was huge.

We went to Canada twice for tournaments. There was big prize money in the Canadian Tournaments. The second time, we won the tournament and the $1,500 first place money. I was chosen as the most valuable player of the tournament. I brought the Canadian paper home, and the manager's wife accidentally sent the article to a friend. Hence no scrape book article.

We played the Harlem Globetrotter's baseball team. Oscar Trouseth was the manager and he was like a second father to me. He and his wife treated me like I was their son. I stayed in their home and they fed me, which was part of the agreement for me to play at Worland. Oscar told me he wished his only child Jack was more like me.

Jack was a great guy, but had some bad habits. Due to a small house and the number of people living there, it was necessary for Jack and me to sleep together in a double bed in the basement. Jack had been in the Army during World War II and had seen a lot of combat. Sometimes he had nightmares about his war experiences that involved people trying to hurt or kill him. Whenever he had a bad dream, he would get very restless and bump me and I would wake up. I would turn on a light and he would come right out of his dream and get angry at himself for having those dreams.

One time, he was standing on the bed and pushing against the basement ceiling with his hands. The mattress was almost touching the ground where his feet were pushing toward the floor. I had slid to the low place in the middle of the bed. He hollered to me that he would hold the roof up until I got out of there. I turned on the light and went back to sleep.

Another time, Jack was against the wall because he thought the ceiling was going to collapse on us. He was telling somebody they weren't going to get him. He always wanted me to be safe, so I never worried.

I really thought the world of that family. Poor Jack suffered from Post Traumatic Stress Disorder, but it was an unknown diagnosis in those days.

During the summer between my junior and senior year, a Dodger tryout camp was held in Worland for two days. I went to it and both scouts liked me. I was the only player they wanted to sign. I told them I wanted a bonus, and they said the best thing would be to send me to spring training in Santa Barbara, California, where they would have time and could evaluate me. They would fly me to Santa Barbara for the only week I was out of school, in between quarters. Then I could meet the university team in Albuquerque when we played our first conference games against New Mexico. When I told Coach Daniels I was considering the offer, he became angry and said that if I went to California, I would not be eligible for any more college games. I wondered if that statement was true.

I don't know if it was against NCAA rules to accept a plane ticket and try out if I didn't sign a contract. I wonder if the NCAA would have found out. I really wanted to go and see how much money the 'big boys' thought I was worth. Being a senior I would have gone and chanced the whole thing for an opportunity to get a bonus, except that I had a stroke of bad luck.

I was working hard during the winter to get into good condition. The weather made it necessary to stay inside. While playing handball, I hit my hand against the wall and dislocated the index finger of my left hand. I couldn't hold a bat, so I decided not to go to California. The Dodgers contacted me and said they had a plane ticket ready for me. In those days, baseball players were told not to lift weights, so the conditioning was totally different than it is now. Many years later the player draft was started for baseball.

Socrates said, "The only thing constant in life is change."

Nowadays, baseball scouts are aware of most good young players beginning in high school or younger. Indoor facilities, pitching machines, strengthening programs, year round work outs, television, video cameras, DVD's, and computers all make it a different baseball world. Better coaching, specialized camps, organized little leagues, nutrition … the list goes on and on. This all makes it so that the players are bigger and stronger than they were before. The metal bats hit the ball harder than the wooden bats do. Professional leagues are the only ones still using the wooden bats. Baseball gloves and all the equipment have been greatly improved. The world has undergone great changes, and baseball is still a great game.

An Autobiography

I loved the game and thought it took more all-round skill to play baseball than any other major sport. You have to be able to run, throw, catch, and hit. Trying to hit a pitched ball that can curve, drop, and travel at different speeds up to 100 miles per hour with a four inch bat is a real challenge. Many sports observers think hitting the ball is the hardest thing to do in any sport.

Gus Angelos completed the season as the leading batter for the Cowboys with a .408 average. Gus had a total of 40 hits and of these 21 were for extra bases. Bob Jingling was next in line with a .348 percentage. He also led the team with stolen bases, pilfering 16 during the campaign.

Physical Prime Time

69

Gus G. Angelos

Decision Time

Throughout my early life, I had very little association with adult men. I never had any grandfathers, relatives or men from church to talk to. In school I never had a male teacher until the fifth grade, and very few in high school. My dad worked all the time. I learned to make decisions for myself. I figured out an interesting way to make big decisions on my own. I would think of a future time and try to figure out where and what I would be doing then. I would then use that as position to try to look backward and evaluate what the best course of action would be – kind of like using hindsight, only before the fact.

I never thought to talk things over with my mother, brother, or anyone. I thought my parents were kind of old fashioned. Sam went into the Military Service and was away for my two years of high school. I wished I would have seen the wisdom and talked over some of my big decisions with a coach or counselor or someone who had experience with similar situations. When you are young, you don't realize that it takes more time than you think to fully mature. One's body matures sooner than one's mind.

After I got married things were different. I had someone else to consider and someone to talk things over with. However, by then many of my big decisions had been made. At the beginning of my senior year at Wyoming, the Air National Guard's Commanding Officer from Cheyenne came to the school and said he wanted a few athletes to join the Guard and eventually become pilots. The Korean War was still on. The colonel said he would promote the athletes so that when they graduated they could go into flight training as officers, not cadets, and then be assigned to the

Guard in Cheyenne. It was a great opportunity and a good way to fulfill your military obligation without going on active duty for two years. I was really interested.

I always wanted to fly, especially jet fighters. It was a difficult decision but I finally decided against it because I still wanted to try for a career as a professional baseball player. Two athletes, who happened to be fellows I had roomed with, signed up with the Air Guard. One cracked up his plane and washed out. He wasn't injured. The other friend completed the first forty-nine flight training phases and then failed to pass a physical exam for jet training. So, he was discharged from the Air Corps and immediately drafted into the Army.

Only other family photo after Sam was married. Taken in about 1951

At the end of my senior year, I had three offers to play more professional baseball. One offer was from the Denver Bears, which was an independent team at that time. The other offers were from the Dodgers and the Cleveland Indians. They all told me they didn't scout much in Wyoming because it had a small population and was located 'out of the way'. That was true in those days.

Slalom race of National Championships at Sun Valley 2011 Age 81

Lake Powell fun 2012

TUESDAY, APRIL 28, 1953. Laramie,

SPORTS SCOPE

BY MIKE CHRISTOPULOS

GRIZZLED GUS ANGELOS, the "pappy" of Wyoming's fledging baseball squad kicked up a clod of dirt as his mates streamed off the diamond following their 11-9 setback at Ft. Warren's hands here last Wednesday.

Gus had just finished staging one of the most vitriolic hitting shows ever seen at the UW diamond—a performance in which three straight times he propelled home runs into the outer reaches of the Poke orchard.

"Obviously I had one of my best days at the plate," the ol' veteran quipped.

"But that was absolutely the worst day in the field I've ever had," he was quick to add.

Though no miscues were charged to the Salt Lake swatter in the official scorebook, Gus was a bit put out with himself for "misplaying" Don Fraley's towering first-inning four bagger.

His concern for his fielding typifies the spirit that may carry Bud Daniel's hirelings to their first conference pennant in a number of years.

This Wyoming baseball team doesn't know when to call it quits. Their last three victories—two over Colorado A & M and a singleton over Ft. Warren—have been come-from-behind affairs which is often the true sign of a champion.

Perhaps one of the most "spirited" kids in the cast is junior leftfielder Fred Schmidt.

He's a real competitor," Wiles Hallock, the Poke tub-thumper declared.

Coach Daniel seconded Wiles' views, pointing out that in the second Aggie tiff, Schmidt threw a perfect "strike" from the outfield to nail a runner charging towards home plate, something

Individual Baseball Records Drop As Result Of A&M Series

Cowboy individual baseball records suffered badly last weekend in their split with Colorado A&M.

Gus Angelos, Wyoming centerfielder, was still leading Poke hitters with a .394 average, quite respectful but still a .32 drop from his average of .426 the previous week. Gus managed only two hits in nine times at bat over the weekend.

Ed Litecky, whose average dropped from .342 to .338 is still the club's second leading hitter, and Fred Schmidt, who lost but one point during the series, is in third with .328.

The three leading batters are also one-two-three in homeruns for the season with seven-six-five respectively.

Angelos still leads the squad in hits with 26, runs with 29, and is tied for the doubles lead with six. Litecky leads in RBIs with 24.

Team fielding is still poor. The Pokes showed five errors in the two game series.

Lefty Thornton Bromley and righthander Al Soroky lead Cowboy pitchers with records of 3-2. Soroky has worked the most innings, 42, leads in runs, 22, and has appeared in the most games, seven.

Bromley is ahead in hits given up, 42, strikeouts, 29, and bases on balls, 28. Bill Fraser shows the best ERA, 2.87.

GUS ANGELOS
Off to good start . . .

Gus Angelos, former South High School athlete, is starring on the Wyoming baseball club this spring.

Gus is majoring in pre-dental work at the Laramie layout and does a right sharp job at the plates—especially home plate.

Gus is wielding a .426 stick in 14 games. His team has won eight and lost six in practice and league games. He has seven home runs.

He should be studying pre-baseball with a record like that.

Gus Angelos No. 1 Cowboy Hitter

Wyoming University batting averages.

	G.	AB.	H.	R.	2b.	3b.	HR.	RBI.	Av.
Angelos, cf	13	48	20	20	4	1	7	20	.417
Lemon, 2b	15	52	20	15	4		3	13	.385
Schmidt, 3b	13	45	15	13	7	1		11	.333
Kosarcich, 1b	13	48	19	17	3	2	2	8	.290
Ostyik, 2b	15	58	14	11	3				.246
Street, c	13	48	11	9					.240
Huelan, ss	13	48	14	13					.220
Gabacia, rf	10	45	15	7	3		1	7	.222
, cf									

Gus Angelos completed the season as the leading batter for the Cowboys with a .408 average. Gus had a total of 40 hits and of these 21 were for extra bases. Bob Jingling was next in line with a .348 percentage. He also led the team with stolen bases, pilfering 16 during the campaign.

Gus Angelos Top Hitter For Cowboys

Center fielder Gus Angelos has supplanted second-baseman Tom Bournellis as the leading hitter on the Wyoming University baseball team.

The sophomore fly-chaser owns a .417 batting average, compared to the .385 mark held by Bournellis.

Angelos has hit safely 20 times in 48 trips to the plate while Bournellis claims an equal number of hits in 52 appearances.

Catcher Bill Wilson is the team's third best hitter with a .380 average. He claims the most number of hits, 22, and also is tops in the RBI department with 18.

The only other regular batting above .300 is third-baseman Keith Pilger who sports a .375 average.

	AB	H	R	RBI	Av
Angelos	48	20	20	16	.417
Bournellis	52	20	15	8	.385
Wilson	58	22	17	18	.380
Pilger	56	21	8	16	.375
Schildgen	49	14	6	11	.282
Allen	48	12	6	8	.250
Hughes	36	7	5	6	.194
Lemons	31	6	10	4	.184
Bandow	37	6	6	1	.162

Angelos' Homerun Gives Pokes Victory Over Ags

Fort Collins, Colo., April 24—Angelos with one more inning homerun by Gus gave Wyoming a 4-3 win over Colorado A&M in a Skyline conference game.

Buffs Nip Pokes, 13-12

BOULDER, April 28.—(UP)—Colorado University made it nine straight baseball victories here today on a ninth inning single by Don Branby which scored Larry Horine from second base to beat

infield paved the way for seven Colorado runs in the fourth inning to put the Buffs ahead, 10-9. Colorado got only two hits, but one of them was a bases loaded homer by First Baseman Les Rich.

But Pokes Bow to Ft. Warren

Gus Angelos Slams 3 Straight Homers

By MIKE CHRISTOPULOS
Bulletin Sports Editor

In their usual role against their ol' service nemesis, Wyoming started slow and finished fast, but even a superhuman effort by Grizzled Gus Angelos was not enough to haul the Cowboys past favored Ft. Warren here yesterday afternoon.

The Punchers sported the win-

HARLEM GLOBETROTTERS TAKE INDIANS THURSDAY NIGHT AS LOCAL SEASON ENDS

Harlem Globetrotters ended the local baseball season Thursday night by soundly trouncing the Worland Indians 20 to 8.

Indians got off to a fair start, but scored no runs after the fifth inning, while the Globetrotters scored 7 in the second, 6 in the fifth, and 4 in the sixth—to list the bigger stanzas.

Angelos scored two home runs for Worland, and Slade and Douglas rounded the bases for the Globetrotters. The visitors played errorless ball, but Worland ran up a total of nine. Iwakiri replaced Stine on the mound for Worland in the fourth.

Indians	ab	r	h	Globetrotters	ab	r	h
Graham, 2b	4	1	1	Cunningham, cf	5	3	1
Miller, 3b	4	2	1	Redd, 3b	7	1	2
Troseth, ss	2	2	1	Davenport, rf	7	2	2
Angelos, cf	4	3	3	Wheeler, lf	6	1	3
Heron, 1b	4	0	1	Slade, 1b	7	4	3
Parker, c	4	0	1	White, 2b	6	2	1
Hillhouse, rf	3	0	0	Ivory, ss	6	2	2
Davis, lf	4	0	1	Mayes, c	6	3	4
Stine, p	3	0	0	Douglas, p	6	2	2
TOTAL	32	8	9	TOTAL	56	20	20

Errors: Graham (2), Miller (2), Stine, Troseth, Hillhouse and Davis. Umpires: Austin and Gentry.

The best offer I got came from Cleveland. They would send me to Tucson, Arizona for the rest of the summer. The pay would be $350.00 a month. If I was still with the team at the end of the year, I would get a $2,500.00 bonus. I really wanted to give professional baseball another try. I had matured physically but even more mentally and was very confident that I could be successful in the minor leagues. I believe the odds were about 25 to 1 that I could have been a successful big league baseball player. The more I played against better players, the better I performed. I would liked to have known whether I was good enough to be a big league baseball player. Even in my short professional career, I talked to players who claimed they had been taken advantage of and not paid bonus money. I couldn't count on the conditional bonus and desperately needed money for dental school.

The military draft also was a tremendous problem because I would have been called to active duty to serve two years in the fall, had I stopped going to school. I had a commission as a 2nd Lieutenant in the infantry through R. O. T. C. An Army recruiter told me, I could probably play baseball in the Army but I wasn't sure of that because I would be an officer and that could create problems. It definitely would not help my baseball career to put it on hold for two years.

The Worland Indians semi-pro team made me an offer of a guaranteed $1,000.00 per month plus free room and board. I made the decision and went to Worland and had a good season. By the end of the summer, I had saved a little over $3,000.00 to start dental school. I also owned a three-year-old Ford convertible and had no debt.

It was a very difficult decision and a bitter pill for me to swallow to give up professional baseball. Many times through out the years I have wondered what might have been for me had I stayed with professional baseball – many 'what ifs' have crossed my mind, such as, 'What if I would have come along a little later in time when I didn't have to compete against all of the World War II veterans?' and 'What if the scouting and drafting system of today were in place? What if they had rookie leagues? What if student loans were available in those days? What if my parents could have helped me financially? What if the Korean War had never come along and I hadn't had a military obligation?' The list goes on and on.

MOM'S FAVORITE PICTURE OF THE KIDS

Pearl's favorite photo of kids

At any rate, I made my decision and it was time to move along to my next adventure. I always felt bad that my family and friends hardly ever saw me play baseball because I played so little in Utah.

I would receive a $2500 bonus at the end of the season if I was still with Tucson, and $350 a month salary. I wanted the money up front. I had heard that these bonuses were often not paid. I wish I had had some time and money to look everything over. I was entirely on my own, broke, and with no place to stay. I decided to go with the semi pro offer of a guaranteed $1000 a month, plus free room and board. I could also get a job and earn extra money. So I made a decision to go with the money. By the end of the summer, I had saved a little over $3,000 for school. First year tuition was $1800.

Oldest golf brother's foursome in the world. Ages 91-97 Forsgren's Bob on right, James, Keith, and Ferron.

In dental school I played two winter seasons for the Glendale, CA, Pirates at Casey Steingle Field in a semi-pro league, and played well. No money though. Still, it was a good league because the Los Angeles area had so many good players who lived there. Every player on our team was home for the winter and was still playing pro-baseball except me. I batted over three hundred and did well with them, but that was the end of my baseball days.

The team was offered a nice all expenses paid two-week trip to Cuba to play some games and I really wanted to go. I talked to Dean McNaulty of the Dental School. He told me I couldn't miss two weeks of school and that I should make up my mind to either be a dentist or a baseball player. It was just as well because Pearl and Mark would have been alone during that time. As I recall, Pearl was reluctant, but agreed to the Cuba trip. She probably realized it wouldn't come to pass. That was before Castro had gained power in Cuba.

On my way overseas after graduating from dental school and being newly inducted in the Army, I played my last baseball game for a team in Utah that was playing for the Semi-Pro State Championship. I remember I got one hit in three times at bat, and we won the game. Clair Bailey was on leave from the Air Force and also played that game. Kent Peterson, a ten-year major league pitching veteran, was managing and pitching for the team. Kent was a friend who grew up a block from my house. That was the summer of 1957. I really loved playing baseball and will forever be grateful for what it did for me. In my younger years it gave me great enjoyment, gave me good friends, and kept me out of trouble. In the years since I was a competitive baseball player some things have changed in the game. A few rules have been changed, such as the strike zone is a little smaller than it used to be. Protective helmets are required. More umpires are used in each game. Aluminum bats were invented and are now used at all levels of baseball, except in professional leagues. The aluminum bat doesn't break like wooden bats and hits the ball harder so that the ball goes farther than with a wooden bat. I never used a metal bat when I was playing baseball. They hadn't been invented.

As a young boy, frequently we used broken wooden bats that we taped up because we didn't have any money to buy new bats. The various skills required to be a good baseball player, such as run, throw, field, and hit the ball, haven't changed. The players are bigger and stronger than they used to be. Coaching and year round training to strengthen and develop skills are better. In my era, there were no indoor facilities so we only played in the spring and summer. Baseball fields are much better and baseball gloves have been improved. Young players train year round and have good conditioning programs. Fewer players participate in more than one sport in high school. I was a good student of the game and got to know it well. I have often wondered if I ever would have gone to college if it hadn't been for baseball.

Years later, I played in three or four "Old Timers" games. The " Old Timer" games were older men who had played some professional baseball. Usually, it was a few innings played before a regular professional league game. It was a promotional thing. That was fun, even though everyone playing was considered 'over the hill'. Now they have many short entertainment productions at games to keep the fans' attention.

I continued to play fast pitch softball and slow pitch softball until I was 71 years of age. A few last thoughts about my baseball career. I was always one of the leading hitters on any team I ever played on. I should have gone back to playing an infield position in high school. I was as big as the average big league infielder and that makes things better. I believe that I had the skills to be a good infielder. I wasn't ready to be a professional baseball player at the age of seventeen. I believe I would have done much better had I waited a year or two longer to play. However, that is part of life – to live and learn.

The last thing I have to say about baseball is about something that happened around 1975. A Yankee Scout with twenty years' experience passed through Salt Lake City. He phoned me and we went out to dinner. He then came to our house. His name was Gus Poulos. We had played on the same team and against each other for four years when I was in college and he was in the Air Force. He told my son, Craig that I was good enough to have become a major league player. I didn't ask that question. Gus (the baseball scout) went on to say that with the expansion of the number of teams in the big leagues, and the drain of player talent into professional basketball and football, I was good enough. I asked him to be absolutely honest and not just say things that I would like to hear. He said that it was "the absolute truth." I will never know, but it was a nice dream and a good thought.

After I made the decision to not play professional baseball anymore, I decided everything else that I would do athletically would be for fun, and as a hobby. That has been the case. It has proved a bonus because I had been exercising a great deal – before the days that doctors decided it was so beneficial for health. I firmly believe that exercise and sports activities have made a large contribution to my being able to do many physical activities and enjoy good health during my senior years. I loved sports and especially baseball. Those activities helped to keep me active and connected with friends when I was young, and contributed to a happy childhood. Baseball gave me a chance to travel extensively throughout the United States and in Canada. It was responsible for my going to college, and eventually going into dentistry. It was great fun and taught me many lessons about sportsmanship, hard work, discipline, cooping with defeat, frustration, teamwork, setting goals, and on and on. I loved it. It was also a time when no steroids or performance drugs were available, so everyone came to play on even terms.

Playing was always much more fun that watching baseball. Now I like college football on TV the best.

Gus G. Angelos

More College Days and Career Choices

There is more to life than athletics. So, I will go back and write about some of the other events that took place during my college years. During those years I made some of the biggest decisions in my life. This is probably true for most people during the years between fifteen through twenty-five.

Upon arriving at the University of Wyoming, I was given two days of entrance exams. The exams were developed at Ohio State University. The tests were general knowledge and I. Q. type tests. Evidently some of the tests dealt with emotional stability. I was informed of this two years later when I changed majors.

As previously noted, I was assigned an advisor who asked me what I want to study and what career I wanted to pursue. I hadn't really given a lot of thought to either of those questions because I never thought I would go to college. I decided that I wanted to be a coach and be able teach in high school. My advisor thought it would be helpful if I could teach other subjects besides physical education. Even though I hadn't taken a lot of science classes in high school, I liked science, so I choose biology for a major. I honestly didn't know if I could pass the college classes because I hadn't taken any college preparation classes in high school.

My schedule the first quarter was botany, English, physical education, R.O.T.C., history, and an education class. Come the end of my first quarter, I had two A's, and B's or C's in rest of my classes, except for a D grade in American History. I had an outstanding American History professor named Gail McGee, who later became a Senator from Wyoming for nearly eighteen years.

He gave a weekly test of twenty-five very tricky true-false questions. The midterm and final exams had 100 true-false questions. There was two exchange students who sat on my row: one girl from Germany and one girl from Sweden. Both always scored very well on the tests. I couldn't figure out how foreigners could do better in U. S. history than me.

After the first quarter was over and I had my D, I found out that all Professor McGee's test questions were on file at the Fraternities and Sororities. Everyone else in the class had access to the questions but me. Everyone just studied the questions the night before the weekly tests. That made it very easy to answer the questions and get good grades. I asked the girl who sat next to me if I could come and study the questions with a group at her sorority house each Thursday evening. She said, "yes" and from then on, it was a breeze to take those tests and get good grades. I was very happy to find out I could get satisfactory grades in college.

Professor McGee really sparked my interest in history.

The Korean War started the summer after my first year of college in 1950. Not knowing what was in the future with another war, I went to spend a couple of months in Salt Lake City. I worked at the brickyard and played baseball.

I had only seen a dentist two times in my life previously, but was getting smarter and soon realized I had better do something soon in order to avoid painful dental problems later. The first time I ever saw a dentist was when I was four years of age with an abscessed baby tooth. I remember I was put to sleep and had a nightmare during the time the tooth was removed. Mother took me on the streetcar to the dental office and we took a taxi home. I guess I was still groggy from the anesthetic so mom carried me into the house.

The second visit to the dentist was when I was twelve years old. A new tooth grew into my mouth, completely crowding out of line with the other teeth. On that occasion, at age twelve, I was sent to the dentist alone on the bus by mom. The old streetcars were gone and Salt Lake City had nice buses. The dentist removed the tooth and filled some teeth. I will always remember the dentist standing over me while showing me the tooth he just removed. The bloody tooth had a sharp curve on the root and he was smiling and happy because the tooth had not broken. It was another bad experience for me. I never wanted to see a dentist again for the rest of my life.

An Autobiography

At age twenty, I could see in a mirror that I had some cavities in my teeth and knew something needed to be done or else I would have painful teeth. I decided I needed to see a dentist while I was home. I didn't know a dentist in Salt Lake City, or anywhere else for that matter. My sister, Margaret, had braces on her teeth and the orthodontist, Dr. Joel Gillespie, was a big sports fan. He always told Margaret that he wanted to meet me because I was a college athlete at the University of Wyoming. During that period of time the University of Wyoming was the real athletic powerhouse in this area of the country.

Joel & Barbara Gillelspie

I went to see Dr. Gillespie, hoping I could get a free exam and save some money. Dr. Gillespie was very nice and took a look in my mouth then told me I had a problem similar to my sister's and that I should have braces.

I remember looking up at him from the chair and saying, "Doc, I can't afford braces. The only reason I'm going to college is because I have a scholarship." I didn't even know enough to address him as 'doctor'.

He said, "Follow me around, and lets talk about sports."

I followed him around and saw that his work was very interesting. After about twenty minutes, Dr. Gillespie stopped, turned to face me, and then said, "I'll tell you what … if you pay for the materials, I will do the work for free."

I was absolutely astounded to hear an offer like that when I had just met the man. I asked him how much money that would be and I think he said around $350.00. I told him he was on.   During the next couple of weeks, he removed three teeth, did a few fillings, and put the braces on my teeth. I came home once a month for the next two years for the appointments. My two upper cuspids (eye teeth) were very crowded and looked like fangs on an animal. All of my teeth were crowded and I was always very self conscience about my mouth.

I contacted Dr. Gillespie in 2010 and asked him why he made such an offer after knowing me for only thirty minutes. He told me he wanted to think about it and would phone me back after a week, which he did.

Joel Gillespie just turned ninety but he was still sharp as ever and fun to talk to. He said he had Greek friends while growing up in Tooele, Utah. Some played high school football with him and were close friends. Joel knew that my name was Greek and he knew a little about me from my sister. In those days, he had season tickets to the University of Utah's football and basketball games and was very intrigued by the set plays the Wyoming' s basketball team used. He asked me about things like that at our first visit.

When Joel phoned me back, he said that I was a very 'likable person' and that he felt a real bond immediately. He also said that there had to be a spiritual element involved, which he could not explain.

Joel's offer and treatment totally changed my life. I have thanked him many times for doing that. During my second year in college, Dr. Gillespie continued to encourage me to think about dentistry and orthodontics as a career. I thought it over that entire year and decided to go for it. I will always be indebted to Dr. Gillespie for the encouragement and generosity he gave me. He planted the idea in my head to become an orthodontist.

At the beginning of my third year, I transferred from the College of Education to the Liberal Arts College. I immediately got a letter to report to the Dean of the School of Education. He was an Ivy League Ph.D. who only stayed at the University for a couple of years. I don't remember his name. He asked me why I had decided to give up teaching and I told him. He said he was very sad to see good people leave the education field. He then told me about the entrance exams I had taken. He showed me the scores on the emotional stability exams. My lowest score was 88 percentile and the remaining scores were in the 90's up to 99. He said he thought that I 'must be the best adjusted and most stable college student' he had come across. That was very interesting to hear.

During my third year, my classes were very difficult. I was the only person in my physics, advance math, and chemistry classes that had never taken any of those subjects in high school. To make matters more difficult, I had to take math and physics with the engineering students, due to scheduling conflicts. I even got a waver to take a physics course before I had studied trigonometry. Students just didn't take those classes together the same year.

Engineering students had more detailed and more difficult math and physics classes than the pre-med and pre-dental students. I thought I might as well go for it, thinking that if I could pass those classes with decent grades, then I probably had enough brainpower to get through dental school. I passed everything, but never got better than a "C" in chemistry. I managed "B's" and "C's" in the other science classes.

Physical education and military subjects (ROTC) always brought "A's" for me, which helped my GPA (grade point average). In one organic chemistry class, a good friend Ray Gossett, who had been a scholarship football player and quit to become a pharmacist, was my lab partner. He said I had talked him into becoming a dentist rather than a pharmacist and was forever grateful for that. I also suggested he ask a girl in the class to a dance when he told me he didn't know who to ask. At first he said he didn't think she was very cute and didn't want to ask her. He finally did take her to the dance and wound up marrying her. Ray became an outstanding dentist in Riverton, Wyoming. He even become a member of the State Board of Dental Examiners, which is quite an honor.

My fourth year was somewhat easier, especially after I had been accepted to dental school. During my last quarter at the University of Wyoming, I took the classes that I wanted to and that would prepare me for dental school. I would miss quite a few days of schooling due to baseball travel each spring quarter. That was a relaxed quarter.

I did not receive a Bachelors Degree. I had about 235 units of credit. One needed about 205 for a degree. I needed two years of a foreign language for a Bachelors Degree in Liberal Arts or I needed to student-teach to get a degree in education. I did complete a major in physics-chemistry and a minor in zoology and botany. I also had a minor in military science. I always wanted to take two years of German, but R.O.T.C. made that impossible.

I joined the Sigma Chi Fraternity in the middle of my first year at Wyoming strictly because my mother wanted me to belong to a Fraternity. I think Mom must have read or heard something that made her think that being in a fraternity was a wonderful college experience. Mother never

UNIV OF WYOMING - 1953

My Sigma Chi Sweetheart

made requests, especially like that one.

I should have waited to join the fraternity. The athletic dorms were like a fraternity because we all lived together, ate together, and were athletes together as best friends. Fraternities and sororities were a good thing on Wyoming's campus because Laramie was such a small town. It was cheaper and one had better living conditions if you lived in a fraternity or sorority house, rather than the dormitories at that time.

Mom offered to pay the initiation fee, so I joined, mainly for her. I benefitted by forming a few good friendships. I had a wonderful time at the University of Wyoming. I would have preferred to stay in Salt Lake City and gone to college there, but it didn't work out that way. I also think it might have been better for my baseball career to have played college ball first, rather than go professional at age seventeen.

During my college years, the only other honor I thought would be nice to achieve – besides an education – was to be the President of the "W" Club, which was a club for varsity letter athletes (no sports programs for women in those days). I also wanted to become a member of "Who's Who in American Universities and Colleges." I was able to achieve both of these honors. Additionally, I was a member of the student senate for two years.

The senate experience was interesting. I was on one committee that was responsible to arrange for a big student dance. I helped obtain a nationally known band for the dance. Big bands didn't play in little college towns, especially in wide-open spaces like Wyoming. We lucked out and got Les Brown and his Band of Renown, which was touring the U.S.A. They were traveling through Wyoming back to Chicago. It really took a big chunk of money from student funds –something like $1,600.00 for one

Ft. Benning, Georgia 1952 Gus Top Right

night – but it was a big deal to have a big time band at the school.

I believe these extra curricular activities, along with athletics, helped me get into dental school.

During my younger years, I wasn't interested in student politics or offices, except maybe to be a captain of an athletic team. In my day, being captain meant you were one of the better players – a coach appointed position. I never sought any of these positions in college.

I was also the vice president of my dental school class my last year. I think a lot of those positions are popularity contests. However, they can be good experiences to help you grow, and they look good on a resume.

Once in a while I could afford to go to a movie. I never once ate anything in town, except on rare occasions when I would go out to get a milk shake. There were very few things to do in the town of Laramie. They had lots of bars, one bowling alley, and two movies theaters. My entertainment was to go to all the athletic events and some of the university entertainment events.

I went to a talk given by President Harry Truman on campus, which was very nice. I never had access to watch television. I was invited to go to four close friends' homes during my four years at Laramie. I enjoyed that and went to Sheridan, Riverton, Cheyenne, (towns in Wyoming) and a little farm town in western Nebraska.

There was only one radio station in Laramie that played mostly cowboy music. I got tired of that. At night you could get lots of radio stations. We used to listen to KVOO from Tulsa, and KSTP from Minneapolis. They both had good music. Two times I wrote the Tulsa station and requested they play "The Sweetheart of Sigma Chi" when Pearl was in Laramie for the annual sweetheart dance. The stations came through at the time requested and Pearl and I listened together.

Pearl came to Laramie three times in February for the yearly Sigma Chi Sweetheart Ball. The first time, the Greyhound bus was stalled for several hours when the highway was closed for snowdrifts. After that she flew. Her sister, Joy came once with her, and my sister Margaret also. My social life at school was very limited. I didn't have the money or desire to socialize much and I had my own busy agenda. There were four boys to one girl attending the university. There were 3,000 students. The girls really had a great social life as they were in short supply and had no competition from town girls. In my opinion, most of the girls were not very attractive. I believe many high school girls married young in the small towns around the state and many choose to go to schools away from Wyoming.

The Korean War prompted a lot of guys who didn't go to college to get married early to change their draft eligibility status. Pearl has never let me forget a remark I made to her one time when I said that she 'could have been a Queen at the University of Wyoming'. She teased me for years, quoting me as saying to her, "Even you! could be a Queen at Wyoming." She missed the point. Pearl was very pretty, everybody thought so, and especially me.

R.O.T.C.
Reserve Officer Training Corps

T he University of Wyoming is a land grant school. In 1862 during the Civil War, a law was passed that would grant each state federal land for a state university. One requirement by the Federal Government was that all able bodied male students were required to take two years of R.O.T.C. If one was a veteran or physically unfit, one could be exempt. I didn't want to do that but had no choice.

The United States did not draft anyone between World War II and the Korean War. When the Korean War began, they were really caught shorthanded and had to mobilize again to draft large numbers of men my age. It was possible to get a deferment to finish college by taking a college deferment exam. I was told by my draft board in Salt Lake City that the exam probably wouldn't help me because so many men from Salt Lake City were on LDS missions and already had deferments. I decided not to interrupt college and so I voluntarily took the third and fourth year of R.O.T.C., which deferred me from the draft. This was a big problem, as it required taking lots of military classes. It also meant that between my third and fourth year, I would be required to go to Ft. Benning, Georgia for six weeks of infantry training. This translated to less baseball, less work, and less income over the summer. Looking back, I should have taken the college deferment test, and taken my chances.

I never wanted to avoid serving my Country. I believe I still would have been called into the Army as a dentist. Infantry training was really stepped up and concentrated when the U.S. was at war. I didn't mind the hard work.

At summer camp, we did the typical things such as marching drills, obstacle courses, crawling under live machine gun fire, learning and shooting many types of infantry weapons, bivouacs over night, forced marches, maneuvers, class work, and demonstrations. I did well with the weapons and would have qualified for quite a few sharp shooter medals had I been on active duty. Later, when I was in the Army, I was the only one stationed at the hospital that received a sharp shooter's medal. I still have it. The only weapon that you could qualify with as a dental officer was the old Army 45 caliber revolver.

I had an interesting experience at Ft. Benning. One evening all 3,500 cadets were taken to an area for a demonstration. We were shown the firepower of a reinforced rifle company. The tracer bullets made it a very impressive presentation when dark. We were also shown a paratrooper jump of the 81st Airborne. When it was time to leave the area, I went to my assigned large truck and took a seat on the back of the truck. After everyone of our group was loaded, the tailgate of the truck was closed. An active duty staff Major came to the back of the truck and said something. I did not hear him because there were about 150 big 2 ½ ton trucks with the motors running causing a great deal of noise. It turned out that an R.O.T.C. cadet from MIT (Massachusetts Institute of Technology, one of the most prestigious schools in the country) couldn't find his truck. The officer was telling me to move down to let the fellow ride back to the barracks with us. When I understood what was wanted, I moved and didn't think any more about it.

All of the cadets had their names printed on their steel helmets. Unbeknown to me the officer was unhappy with me. The next morning at roll call, I was ordered to report to my company commander. I had been reported for disobeying a direct command from the previous night. That is a serious thing in the 62 Army. I told my C.O. what had happened. To this day, I don't know if he believed me, but I think he disliked me for some reason. He didn't know me any better than he knew any of the other 120 cadets in my company. The only thing I could ever figure out was that he was a career officer from the 'Deep South' and some southern men had a real prejudice against blacks, Catholics, and Jews. With my last name, perhaps he thought I was Catholic. For all I know, he may have looked at my records and been prejudice against Mormons. The fifties were different days before the Civil Rights Movement.

An Autobiography

Nothing more happened at summer camp, but I think it became part of my R.O.T.C. summer camp records that were sent back to Wyoming. When I got back to school, I had reason to believe that I would be called to be one of the top student commanders. I was not. I was called to be the first company commander. This gave me better experience to actually command about 100 cadets rather than have a staff position, so I wasn't disappointed.

A couple of other interesting experiences in regards to R.O.T.C. happened. The Army gave a general I. Q. Test to all the men at the university who were taking R.O.T.C. A few weeks after the test, one of the staff officers told me he was surprised that I had one of the top five scores in the school. My score was around 133. I was pleasantly surprised. During the fall of my last year, five senior students were call to the R.O.T.C. office and told to report in a class-A uniform. While together in the office, we were asked some questions and interviewed. We were told about the 175th anniversary celebration of West Point. Two men from the group were to be selected to go to West Point with expenses paid by the government. We were told to wait outside the office for a few minutes while a decision was made.

One of our football coaches, Coach Kaufmann, had been in the Army Reserve and been called on active duty due to the Korean War. Thanks to some big time political help from Wyoming's senators, he got stationed at the university and continued to coach. After a few minutes, Major (coach) Kaufman came out of the office and kicked me hard in the seat of my pants. I was really surprised and asked him why he had done that. He took me to the side and told me if I would have had a recent haircut and shined my shoes, I would have been chosen to go to West Point. He really wanted an athlete to represent the university. That was another lesson I learned in the 'school of hard knocks'. With hindsight, I think it would have been a great experience to go to West Point, especially with the Army footing the bill. I never did get very enthused about military spit and polish things.

I received a commission as a 2nd Lieutenant in the Army Reserve in June of 1953. Later that year, the Korean War came to a conclusion. New Infantry Lieutenants had a high casualty rate in Korea. I don't think I would like to have been involved in combat because of the timing when the war ended, but I was ready to go to war for this great country.

Gus G. Angelos

Getting Accepted
Into Dental School

D ental schools were very difficult to get accepted into during that period of time. The great number of veterans that went to school after the war created a problem, as the dental schools could not increase their enrollment for several years. It was necessary to write individual schools to make separate applications with each one (no computers fax machines, or copiers).

Sadly, the Wyoming faculty didn't have a lot of experience helping students get into dental school. The state of Wyoming had an agreement with the state of Colorado and could select and send two medical students each year to attend medical school at the University of Colorado. I wished in a way that I would have tried to get into medical school because I was told I would have been selected.

Each dental school wanted a detailed application, transcripts of grades from high school and college, two letters of recommendation from professors, and two other letters from other people that would address character and personal qualifications of each applicant. They also wanted a photo. You also had to arrange for your DAT (Dental Aptitude Test) score to be sent to each school as well. Each school required some money to process your application.

At that time no dental schools were located in any of the 'mountain states'. There were schools on the west coast, while all the other schools were located between the Midwest and the East Coast. I made applications to the following schools: St. Louis University, Washington University in St. Louis, Creighton, University of Nebraska, Western Reserve, University of Kansas, University of California, and University of Southern California. The applications needed to be mailed out a year in advance.

I wanted to do everything possible to get accepted, so I decided to go to as many schools as possible, make interview appointments, and look the schools over. Only Southern Cal wanted an interview, which I will write about later.

I talked my friend, Ray Gossett into going with me during Thanksgiving week. I felt I could miss three days of school. I never missed a day of school due to illness. I don't think I ever missed even a day or class except for this trip and a trip to L. A. for an interview. I was required to miss several school days for baseball games in Colorado and New Mexico, which made it difficult to make up the work in the science labs. There was always the constant pressure to get good grades.

One of our fraternity brothers offered his parents' house in Omaha for an overnight stay to help with expenses. His dad was a minister and they really treated us nice, including a nice dinner. We drove my car to Omaha, to Kansas City, and then to St. Louis. On the way back we got caught in a blizzard and the roads were closed. This caused us to miss going to the University of Nebraska.

Our interview at the University in St. Louis was really an interesting experience. The dean's secretary told us he would squeeze us in for five minutes only because he was 'very busy and we didn't have a confirmed appointment'. It turned out that he was a wonderful southern gentleman who had roomed with a fellow from Wyoming for four years when they were in dental school. The Wyoming man became a senator from Wyoming.

The dean and senator had remained close friends and had hunted and fished together many times. The dean reminisced for an entire hour about their friendship. We hardly said a word. The last couple of minutes he asked us why we wanted to be dentists. We gave him a quick answer. The dean then put his arms around us and walked us all the way to the front door and said he had 'never had such a fine interview with two such outstanding young men'.

Weeks later, we both got accepted at his school. After the snowstorm passed over Nebraska, and the roads were opened, it was Thanksgiving Day. I decided to continue driving from Laramie to Salt Lake City to surprise everyone. It was always fun to go to Salt Lake.

Two weeks later, Southern Cal. requested an interview, which was to be held in December. I wrote to tell them I couldn't make it. Jack Preston, a friend I knew from some classes we had taken together, came rushing to my dorm a few days later. Jack's brother who had graduated from USC's dental school, and lived in Redlands, California said we would never be accepted if we didn't go for an interview. Jack's brother sent him money for the train trip.

Another pre-dental student, whose father worked for the railroad, had a free railroad ticket and they were both going for an interview. Airplane travel was way too expensive in those days for students. Jack and the other fellow told me if I wanted to drive my car we could share expenses. I told them no. They said if I changed my mind they would still go. I thought about it overnight and went to my eight o'clock class the next morning. While in my class and at the very last minute, I decided to go. I made it to the railroad station about fifteen

Ennis Star and Harvard Ward Team
Gus 2nd from right standing

minutes before the train was to leave. The three of us drove 1200 miles to Los Angeles and stayed overnight with Jack's brother. Next morning, Jack's brother drove us to the school for our twenty-minute interviews. There were five men on the committee who interviewed me. One of the men told me that he could see from my records that I was an athlete and the USC had lots of dumb jocks. He asked me if I fit in that category. Later I found out that he said things like that to many of my classmates during their interviews. I think he tried to shake people up to see how they handled pressure. There were over 800 applicants for 100 freshman slots at USC's dental school. Remember, no electronic means were available to file multiple applications in those days. So students generally applied to fewer schools.

During the Christmas vacation of 1952, I got a job selling Christmas trees at Allied Surplus store in Salt Lake City. On Christmas Eve, the boss said to me and another college guy that if we wanted to stay until after six p.m., we could keep any money we took in selling trees. I stayed until about eight p.m. and then went home. My mother fixed supper for me and told me I had a letter. The letter turned out to be one of the best Christmas presents I have ever received. It was my first acceptance letter – to dental school at Washington University in St. Louis.

I sent most of the money I had saved on that vacation ($50.00) for the non-refundable acceptance fee. I waited to send the acceptance fee until I returned to Laramie so I could see if I had an acceptance from USC as well. I had decided I would get the best education at USC, and I liked California better as the location for my next home.

As I drove on the campus, I saw Jack Preston waving an envelope and yelling at me. I stopped as Jack showed me his acceptance letter to USC. Jack was a brilliant young man who always wanted to be a dentist. He went to summer school and only had two years of pre-dental. I think schools had a policy to sort through their applicants and send out acceptances to the most outstanding applicants first before they then worked down the list.

I had hoped my extra curricular activities and a special letter from the University of Wyoming's President of the Board of Trustees would make up for my B grade point average. The President of the Board of Trustees knew me quite well and was a real baseball fan. He had seen quite a few baseball games, and he liked me. Unfortunately, I did not have any other acceptances waiting for me at my mailbox at school.

During the next few weeks I did receive five additional acceptance letters and finally got the desirable one from USC. I wrote to the four other schools, where I had been accepted, and told them I had already accepted another school's position. I also wrote the other two schools I had not heard from, asking them not to consider me anymore. The other fellow who drove to L. A. never did get accepted to any school.

I now had a big hurdle behind me. The next was to see how baseball, the Army, and Dental School were going to work out. I also needed to pass my last organic chemistry class, which wasn't easy because I had missed so much school playing baseball.

Gaining a Testimony and Getting Married

Gus & Pearl - September 9, 1953

Wedding Day With Both Parents

Mother sent us three children to the LDS Church once in a while with the other children on our street when we were small children. It was not on a very regular basis. I remember going to Liberty Ward as a little guy, which was about a half mile away, and attending the ward shows and sometimes primary. Harvard Ward was built in 1937, when I was seven years old. I remember playing in the building when it was under construction. I went there once in a while for Sunday school. As we got a little older, Sam and I got lazy and didn't go to church. Margaret did better than Sam and me.

The kids on our block were good kids and it was a good neighborhood. Most of my friends were Mormons. The Church had basketball teams for boys fourteen years and older – I loved that. When I was fourteen years old, the neighborhood boys and I played basketball for Harvard Ward. We didn't realize it at the beginning of the season, but we had a good team. Ennis Star was a wonderful man. He was our youth leader and coach. I knew and liked him better than any other man in the Ward.

We played basketball, and our team won the Liberty Stake championship. We then went to the inter stake league tournament and won that. We wound up in what was called the All Church Tournament with sixteen teams. We won the first game by two points then won the second game by two or three points. The third game was against Edgehill Ward, who eventually won the tournament. We lost that game by three points, but I will always remember we came back strong. I even made a basket, which was not counted because it scored as the buzzer went off.

The final night we played for third or sixth place. A photographer from the Desert News took my picture before the game. We lost that game in overtime and came in sixth place. I made honorable mention on the All Church Team. Had we won third place, I was told I would have made first team All Church. I was a so-so basketball player for school teams, but a good player on Church teams.

An incident took place that season that taught me another of life's lessons the hard way. Our team voted on a captain, which was an honorary position. We had seven players that participated in the voting. Wayne Swenson and I were the only ones nominated. I thought when friends were involved, the customary thing to do was to vote for the other person and he would vote for you. It turned out I lost four to three because Wayne voted for himself and I also voted for him.

I remember playing the accordion once in sacrament meeting when I was about twelve years old. I played a march and thought it was a lot of work to walk to church and carry the accordion a half-mile to play for people I didn't know. I mentioned earlier that Sam and I were baptized in the LDS Church, but I seldom attended church. The year I played basketball, it was necessary to attend four meetings a month to be eligible to play. I went to the four meetings during that basketball season.

After high school I was ineligible to play church basketball because I had played professional baseball. I was disappointed about that. My baseball friends and I played for the First Methodist Church basketball team in a city league. After I met Pearl and we starting going together, she encouraged me with the Church. She and her family were a great example of LDS values and how one's life could be affected by religion.

As I matured, I started to see a bigger picture of what life was about. I realized a need for religion in my life. I started going to the Institute at the University of Wyoming.

Best Room Mate ever

I even accepted my first church job to be an assistant in the Institute Sunday School. I gave my first talk there. I had been to services at the Greek Orthodox, Catholic, Episcopalian, and Methodist Churches. I liked the LDS services the best, so I started learning more about Mormonism. Mormon doctrine had better answers to my questions than the other religious doctrines. I had never read very much in the Bible, nor had I read the Book of Mormon.

Over a period of time, I developed a small testimony, which has grown over the years. After a couple years in college, I knew I wanted to marry a Mormon girl. The summer before I got married, I did some earnest praying about whether I should marry Pearl. I decided I would marry Pearl and do so in the Temple. It was the right decision, and she was willing to have me as her Husband. We had gone together five years. Most

101

of the time I had been away, so we wrote many letters. It would have been better to do more things together and become better acquainted during our dating years, but it didn't happen.

Pearl and I had a lot in common. We were both first generation Americans, grew up in Salt Lake under similar economic conditions, and attended the same high school. She was a very pretty girl with a good head on her shoulders. She was thrifty and managed her life well. Pearl was good with music and was just a good all-American girl. She was extremely strong in the Church and had a very outstanding family. We had the same value system and goals.

Pearl loved watching baseball games and other sports. I had hoped she would participate more in sports activities after we were married. Girls' school sports were non-existent in those days. Asthma was a problem for Pearl, which held her back, especially in cold weather.

Beach party with dental school friends, Mark, Pearl, Gus holding Sue

Other than asthma, Pearl was healthy and smart. It was a good choice to marry Pearl and she has been a good wife and mother.

When we got married I was three weeks shy of being twenty-four years of age. Pearl was four weeks from being twenty-two years old. That was older than most couples that got married at that time in this country. The average age for girls to marry was around nineteen and for boys, it was around twenty-two that they were married.

Elder Mark E. Peterson, an Apostle, married us in the Salt Lake Temple on September 9th, 1953. Elder Peterson was a good friend of Pearl's parents. Pearl paid all the wedding expenses. We had a large reception held at Lincoln Ward. We stayed two days in Salt Lake City and then took off for Los Angeles to start dental school.

I had all of my possessions in my 1050 Ford convertible. We took all of the wedding gifts, anything we thought we needed to set up a household, plus Pearl's clothing, loaded up the car, and off we went. The rest of the gifts were left at the Trauffer's house.

We stayed overnight at Uncle Nick's house in Los Vegas. He wanted to see us and help us save money. It wasn't a good decision on my part to stay at Uncle Nick's, but Pearl went along with it. The house was dusty and not very appealing for a new bride. The next night we stayed in a cute motel in Santa Ana close to a famous horse race track. Early the next morning we drove to L. A. and got off the freeway close to USC. We had a map but didn't really know our way around. All I knew was that USC was close to the coliseum exit. It was Sunday morning and we looked in the phone book to find the nearest LDS church in the area. We lucked out because the church was only a mile away, and we were just in time for Church.

Gus G. Angelos

A New Room Mate and Dental School

T he Sunday School teacher asked everyone to introduce themselves. It turned out that there were lots of students, including one other new and one second year dental student in the class. Before the day was over, we had been invited to dinner, a ward member helped us find an apartment next to Church, and we had made new friends for the next four years.

Our friends were mainly students at USC who became our family away from Salt Lake City. They were the Ottesens, Jones, Brinks, Gibbons, Shells, Tanners, Evans, and a few others. The second year dental student, Stan Jones offered to pick me up the next morning and take me to the dental school so that I could register. It was a great help because I didn't know my way around and registration had to be done at two different locations on the campus while waiting in lines. It sure would have simplified things if computers had been around in those days.

Parking was always a big problem at USC. I remember writing two checks – one for tuition in the amount of $425.00, and another check for equipment and supplies in the amount of $470.00. Those were for the first semester.

After registration, Stan and I returned to my apartment at noon. Pearl was cleaning, and I asked her to fix us a sandwich. She told me she was busy and for me to do it, so I opened a can of tomato soup and grilled some cheese sandwiches for Stan and me. Later Pearl told me she didn't know how to fix a meal quickly, and especially not for a guest. I never asked Pearl if she knew anything about cooking before we were married. It turned out she didn't know very much, but was very good at reading a cookbook. I've never suffered and she proved to be a very good cook after more than fifty years of preparing meals. Lucky for me, she still enjoys cooking.

A few days later, I took Pearl to the head office of Bank of America and she immediately got a job as a teller. Unfortunately, the job was in the main bank in downtown Los Angeles. She didn't care much for some of the people and nor did she care for the pressure of working in the main office.

The Big Four with wives

Each morning, I drove Pearl to work and then I drove to school. Pearl took the bus home each day. We lived at 147 W. 25th Street. This was the ghetto in the L. A. basin where smog was bad. It was a light commercial area and close to the campus. All the housing was very old and entirely occupied by black people, except for some University students. We settled into a routine: school for me and work for Pearl. I studied every night and Pearl read and listened to the radio. We didn't have a TV.

The first two years of dental school consisted mainly of basic science classes and labs. Subjects such as biological chemistry, anatomy, histology, dental anatomy, oral and general histology, physiology, and lots of dental technique classes with labs filled my days. Students had no choice as to the required subjects they would have to take or to the time of the classes. School went from 8 to 5, Monday through Friday.

There was lots of homework and 105 smart men to compete with. No women. It was a very difficult adjustment for Pearl and I to make one week after getting married. We lived on a very strict budget in our $40.00 per month furnished apartment. In addition, Pearl was away from her family for the first time. Pearl and her three Sisters had all been living at home and the excitement and fast action of life had been exciting and fun. Then the big change came for her to leave family and friends. It was a lonely time for her. Pearl was the first of her sisters to get married.

For me, leaving competitive athletics, no physical exercise, competing academically with 105 smart dental students, and being newly married also made it a stressful period. To complicate our lives more, Pearl became pregnant the first month we were married and had morning sickness for three months. Pearl's grandmother, Gysler died in January, so she flew home for the funeral. The Trauffers paid for the plane ticket. Going home for a short time helped with Pearl's loneliness. She soon realized that she belonged with me in California.

Merl # 4, Gus # 5, and Bill # 6

We spent the holidays with our new friends. We had ward volleyball, basketball, and softball teams, which was our weekly entertainment. This also gave me some exercise. We had some good competition with the Westwood Ward, which had the UCLA students. One year an All American basketball player from BYU played for Westwood Ward. I guarded him and I blocked his first shot and thought maybe he wasn't such a great player. I fouled out of the game trying to guard him. He made five baskets and fifteen free throws to beat us, because of him. He was a very good player and made more points than the rest of his teammates put together.

Our team would practice once a week in the swimming facility that had a small gym at the L. A. Coliseum. This is where the 1932 Summer Olympics Games were held. It was a public facility and was always filled with lots of guys playing basketball. We were the only white players and would always play pick up games with the others there. We never once had any problems with the black players and we generally had lots of fun.

Our ward softball team wasn't too good. It was a fast pitch league and during a play off game an opposing pitcher pitched a one hit game against us. During the game I fouled off a few pitches and he could see I wasn't an easy strike out. I was the only player on our team who didn't strike out in that game.

The pitcher said, "You know I could walk you."

I replied, "It's up to you."

I got a clean hit that time and ruined his 'no hitter' status. It was the only hit our team got that game.

We won our volleyball league and went to a big Southern California Church tournament. We played a Polynesian team and found out we were not very good compared to the guys who had played on the beach their entire lives. They beat us big time. I played on our dental school basketball team for two years whenever we had a team. We won the independent league and had a play off game with the fraternity league champs. The fraternity champs had quite a few athletes that played on USC's varsity teams. They beat us in a pretty close game. During the game I tried to prevent a fast break and had a collision with another player. The other player fell over my back and it looked as if I undercut him. The game was held up while angry fans came onto the floor. The Quarterback of USC's football team came up to me and said words to the effect that he 'should beat me up'. I thought he was going to hit me and I was praying that the fight would be broken up very fast. He was big and mean. Fortunately, he didn't swing. I honestly didn't take a cheap shot and I did apologize to the player who was okay with it. He was a red shirt basketball player.

We would go to the Pacific Ocean beaches for recreation. It was fun and free. I tried to supplement our income with numerous part time jobs. The best job was ushering SC football games for $6.00 per game. I was able to see the games for free. Attending the Notre Dame and UCLA games would be 100,000 fans. We could only afford for Pearl to go to one game a year so she would usually go to the Notre Dame game. Bing Crosby sat in my section once and I saw a few other movie stars at the games.

I found school hard the first year. During Christmas vacation we had lots of big assignments plus we had to study for final exams in January. The grades were posted the only day that I missed in school due to illness.

An Autobiography

One of my friends came by our apartment and told me my grades were all "C's" except for one "B" and one "D" in histology lab. I was one point below the line for a "C" in that class. The one "D" put me on probation for the spring semester. That put a great deal of pressure on me because I would be dropped out of school permanently if I got another "D" during the next semester. That was the policy. No appeals.

I found it very helpful to start studying with a small group of friends. Herm Allenbach, George Gray, Sterling Ottesen, and I became the 'Big Four.' We named ourselves after the big four Allied Country's leaders of World War II. Herm and George didn't live in our ward, but were LDS guys who became my very closest friends; especially George Gray. We would eat our sack lunch together in Exposition Park and study during the noon hour. We would always study together for final exams or for that matter any big exams. Sterling worked part time at an Ice Cream factory as a night watchman and it was okay with his boss if we studied there at night. We could eat lots of ice cream that was not properly wrapped. That was fun.

I did much better the second semester and got off probation. Years later when I was applying to get into an Orthodontic Program, I found out that my class standing was 88th out the 105 students by the end of the first school year. I eventually graduated 52nd out of the 103 in our class who graduated from dental school in 1957. I improved in class standing more than anyone in our class after such a mediocre start. My number in school was #5.

Students were given numbers according to their last name in alphabetical order. We were known more by our number than by our name. Merle Anderson was #4 and Bill Arnett was #6. Chuck Anderson, who was #3 flunked out of school and committed suicide two years later. Chuck had been a dental laboratory technician and was very good with his hands but had a difficult time with the books.

Seats were assigned most of the time. I got to know Merle and Bill very well. Merle was a whiz kid who was four years younger than me, was an excellent student with the books, although naive to some worldly things. Bill Arnett had his own dental lab, was a World Ward II veteran, and was years ahead of the rest of the class when it came to any dental laboratory procedures. Bill was eight years older than me and good at everything

109

in school. His Nephew, Jon Arnett, was an All American running back for the Trojans football team and became a very successful player for the Los Angeles Rams football team. Through Bill, I met and talked with his nephew a couple of times. That was fun.

Everyone came to Bill for help with lab work – even the instructors would talk to him about laboratory questions. There were no women in our class and more than half of our class members were sons of doctors or dentists. All of our close friends were students and most were newlyweds. We had a lot in common.

The only summer vacation we had was between the first and second year. We drove to Salt Lake City and Pearl stayed with her family while I went to Wyoming to work and play baseball. I could make more a lot more money in Wyoming than I could in Utah or California. It was also much cheaper to have a baby in Salt Lake City than Los Angeles.

MARK AT 22 MONTHS IN FIRST STORE BOUGHT SUIT.

Mark Gus Angelos

Pearl's pregnancy was uneventful except for morning sickness for the first three months. She handled everything real well. She worked up to the start of the ninth month. Mark was born ten months after we were married on the 6th of July, 1954. Pearl phoned me in Wyoming as she was leaving to go to the hospital. I immediately drove eight hours to Salt Lake City and stopped at the LDS Hospital to see Pearl and meet Mark. Somehow, the hospital workers forgot to bring our new baby to Pearl after the delivery, so I saw him before Pearl did.

He was a darling baby with lots of dark hair. We brought Mark home and I remember looking at him while he was asleep, and thinking how my life had changed forever. I pondered that Mark would be with us for the next twenty or more years – what a big responsibility that was.

Mark was a perfect baby. I will write about each of our children in a later chapter. After seeing Pearl and Mark, I had to hurry back to Worland for the biggest baseball series of the season against Ft. Warren. This series always made the most money for the team. I took Herb Urry with me because Ft. Warren's baseball team had a lot of left-handed hitters. The manager had asked me if I knew a good left handed pitcher in Salt Lake that I could bring back. Ft. Warren was a team that had all former minor league professional players. The players had enlisted during the Korean War and had special duty playing baseball. Herb pitched very well for about six or seven innings. I remember we won the game. I also remember that I hit a double off the wall and the radio announcer hollered from the broadcast booth the next time I came to bat, and told me that I should hit a home run for my new son. I was very lucky and hit one over the fence.

As I recall we won two of the three games of that series before a big crowd. The ball team bought Herb a ticket to fly back to Salt Lake and paid him some money when he left. Herb and Pearl's sister, Joy planned to get married later that summer. In September, Pearl, Mark, and I went back to our $40.00 apartment and started our second year of dental school. This time Pearl got a better job in the security office of Northrop Aircraft Company in Hawthorne. She worked the swing shift and would leave our house at about four p.m. Our landlady would tend Mark until I got home at about 5:30.

Mark was really a good baby. I had never been around a baby before, which was a new experience for me. I would get him up in the morning and feed him breakfast, change his cloth diaper (no disposables in those days), and put him back in his baby bed. He was very content to play there until Pearl would get up. Pearl always had a sack lunch ready for me to take to school. She would also have something for me to eat for supper. Mark ate baby food at first and later ate the same food as me. He was easy to feed and liked everything.

After school I would take care of Mark and try to study. He wasn't very anxious to go to bed at night and it was better for Pearl's morning schedule if he didn't go to bed too early. It was difficult to do homework while Mark was awake. He was just too lively and wanted me to play with him. He really was an easy guy to manage but the homework came last.

Many nights I remember trying to study after Mark was in bed. I would be so tired. I would read a page of homework and realize that I couldn't remember anything I had just read. As time went by, I found it very helpful to take a short nap and then study. At times I would get up in the middle of the night and study. Usually Mark went to bed around nine p.m.

Pearl and I wrote notes and left them in the bathroom because she would get home around 2 a.m. I was usually sound asleep at that hour. We were fortunate because Pearl rode to work with a group that would pick her up and drop her off right at our door. The travel time was about forty-five minutes. Pearl enjoyed the work and learned a lot about people's history because she helped with security clearances. She said it was the best job she ever had. It was very different from anything she had done in Salt Lake.

It was difficult as newly weds to see each other only on the weekends. Our weekends usually consisted of going to ward ball games on Saturday and going to church on Sunday. In those days there were three different meeting times on Sunday. As time went on, all of our friends had babies, so the new moms had a good time visiting. Each Saturday morning, I would take Mark grocery shopping so Pearl could sleep in. We had envelopes that we would use to put money in for rent, groceries, gas, etc. No credit cards then. Money was really tight. There were no student loans or grants available in those days.

On holidays we would get together with the other students and do something to have fun. We would go to the beach, parks, museums or the zoo, and things like that, which were free.

Studies went better the second year as I got into a routine. After the second year, students went into the clinic building and actually started to work on patients. We still had classes at eight in the morning. Then we would see patients from ten until five. That was very rewarding – to finally start to put all of the academics learned to work on patients. The homework eased up and classes were mainly dental subjects. USC was a very good school, and the education was as good as anywhere else in the USA. I discovered that while I was in the Army and associating with young dentists from all over the country.

Toward the end of our third year, a black man broke into our apartment at about three a.m. He must have seen Pearl come into the house. Pearl heard him break the back screen door and open an unlocked window. She was so frightened she couldn't scream and was whispering in my ear that there was someone in our house. It took me a minute to wake up and it came as a shock to realize that I wasn't dreaming. I could see a black man's face looking in the room through a partially open door. He had a dim flashlight and was looking around. I reacted without thinking and hollered at him to get out. I jumped out of bed and took off after him with the only weapon I could find along the way, which was Mark's cowboy boot.

He got away before I could do battle with him through the window he had opened. Later we laughed about the "weapon" I selected – a two-year-old boy's cowboy boot given to him by his grandparents.

The police responded quickly and picked up a man who had a two-page wrap sheet of burglaries, drugs, and who knows what else. He had dust on him and the police thought he probably was the man who broke into our apartment. Pearl was so frightened that she refused to go to the police car to identify him. I looked at him but couldn't make a positive identification. I asked the police officer what they would do with him. He said they would lock him up for the night and a judge would probably let him go the next day. Pearl wanted to move after that unpleasant experience and because she was pregnant with our daughter, Sue.

We moved to another apartment two blocks north of the Coliseum as soon as we could. The old apartment didn't have a bedroom, only a pull out bed. The new apartment had one bedroom and was much nicer. There were about twelve small apartments arranged in a U-shape with a fence across the front. All the people who lived in the units were students at USC.

A few months prior to that experience, we had accepted a job to manage an apartment in exchange for the rent. It was in a much nicer area of Los Angeles. Pearl looked up the owner of the apartment on the security file at work, and found he was a known Communist. Pearl would have lost her security job at Northrop Aircraft had we worked for a Communist, so we moved back into our old apartment. We had paid the rent until the end of the month.

Two moves in two weeks didn't help the studies. During the time I was a student, I worked as many jobs as possible. They included custodial work at a woolen mill, street cleaning on campus in the dark, cleaning carpets, going to a sanitation plant to test for hearing problems around heavy motor noise, and wrapping bread at Orowheat Bakery. The best job was ushering football games, followed by the bakery job.

I went deer hunting with Stan Jones in Nevada. We shot a deer and used our friend's freezer to store the meat. We also went deep-sea fishing by Tijuana, Mexico and again used the freezer. Any of the three of us who wanted deer meat or fish just took what they wanted. It helped with the food expenses and worked out well.

Sue Angelos

On September 15th, 1956, Sue was born. Pearl again went to Salt Lake City for the birth because of our financial situation. I was very surprised the have a daughter. For some reason, I had always thought I would have a family of only boys. Sue was delightful from "day-one" and has continued to be a wonderful person in every department to this day.

After I first saw Sue, I decided that every man should have a daughter. Sue and Mark became each other's best friend. Pearl and I had an agreement that I would pick the boys' names and she would pick the girls' names. Of course, we both would agree on the final name. When Mark first saw Sue, he couldn't pronounce her name and called her "shoe." At times, I still use that nickname.

Pearl quit work in the last nine months I was in school. We were able to survive financially by selling our car, plus Pearl's parents paid our rent for six months. We even had a date each Friday to go to the 25-cent movie. It was our best year.

We had a few visitors during the four years in school. Pearl's mom and dad came twice. Pearl's Sister Evelyn came to stay with us for a few months, got a job, and also helped with Mark. Pearl's uncle, Al Trauffer came once and took us to dinner at a nice restaurant, which was a real treat. On holidays, we would eat dinner with our friends – each couple would bring some food. We would take turns at each other's apartment. Believe it or not, during our time at USC we went out to dinner one time on our own because of finances. That was to a drive in. Occasionally when we had a vacation and we could afford it, we would drive to Salt Lake. We would drive all night and stop only for gas. Because we would leave after a full day of school, I would get tired in the early hours of the morning and have to take a nap. I never liked the idea of stopping in the middle of nowhere for a nap with the family. I always wanted Pearl to drive part of the way. She didn't want to, so sometimes it was a problem. As time went by, Pearl would drive for an hour to give me a rest. Pearl always said she couldn't sleep in the car, which was a joke because her head bobbed up and down like it was on a spring.

We made several trips, driving all night. This was before the interstate highway system. The distance was 750 miles.

Once on a Christmas vacation, Mark had a bad cold, so we stopped at a motel for the night. The convertible was not a warm car. In the spring of 1957 we took a trip to Fairfield, California to see Joel Gillespie to talk about my practicing with him. The whole area around Fairfield was green and very beautiful. After we moved there, we found out the grass was brown except for a few weeks in the spring. We also took a day trip to San Diego and saw Dr. Bill Bosworth who was in the Navy. Bill's wife grew up in Pearl's ward, and she knew them. It was nice to see that our living standard would move up after completing school.

As time grew near for graduation, we knew I would be called to active duty in the Army. The draft was still in existence and about one third of my graduation class went into the military service.

Graduation day was June 15, 1957 – and I became a real doctor. My Parents

Wonderful day of graduation June 15, 1957

flew to Los Angeles for my graduation. It was a great surprise as they had never taken a vacation and had never flown. It meant a lot to me. Pearl had a beautiful white dress and Sue a pretty pink dress. Mark was three years and Sue almost a year old.

Former United States President, Herbert Hoover's son was the main speaker. It was truly a great day after a long struggle, and we all loved it. I was sworn into the Army that day. My orders for the Army were to report to Ft. Sam Houston in San Antonio, Texas on July 3rd. I had six weeks of basic training before being assigned to a permanent duty station. Pearl and the children stayed with my parents during those six weeks, as her parents were already in Switzerland.

I also had to take a Dental State Board Exam to get a license. I decided to take the California Board. In those days, all of the western states had the board exams during the same week, so applicants could only take one exam each year. I wanted a Utah license, but the California exam was harder to pass and our future location was uncertain because of my desire to become an orthodontist. I took the California board and passed okay. Several years later, things changed, so that one could take regional exams that allowed the applicant to choose which state he wished to practice in.

Our three closest friends, the Grays, the Ottesens, the Allenbachs, and us took a special graduation trip to Sequoia National Park for a few days. Then we started to study for the State Board Exam. Shortly after the exam, the Army picked up our furniture and stored it until we had an active duty assignment. We said goodbye to our friends and started a new chapter in our lives. I have year books from high school, college, and dental school. They bring back many fond memories of events and wonderful friends. One can't live in the past, as life keeps moving forward. So, we always made the best of each new situation. We were happy and excited to finish school. We said goodbye to our friends and L.A.

The Army

We went to Salt Lake where Pearl and the kids stayed with my parents until I finished basic training. In April of that year, 1957, Pearl's father had been called to be the Temple President in Switzerland. It would have been nice had the Trauffers remained in Salt Lake. Then Pearl could have stayed with her parents while in her old neighborhood.

I rode the Greyhound bus to Phoenix, Arizona and was picked up by two classmates, Dick Kindy and Bill King, who were also going to Ft. Sam in Dick's car.

Six weeks of training at Ft. Sam was a breeze. There were about 700 medical doctors and dentists. We learned Army procedures and paper work. In my company formation, I stood next to Joe Baugh and became acquainted with him. We went to church together and had a brief friendship. Ten years later, we became members of an orthodontic study group. We have been close friends now for over forty years.

The Army had us fill out a paper, which asked where we would like to be stationed for our active duty. The paper asked if we wanted an assignment overseas or stateside, and general areas. I requested Germany first. When my orders came at the end of basic training, I was assigned to the 130th Station Hospital in Heidelberg, Germany. I believe it was the best assignment in the entire army. Heidelberg is a beautiful city. It was the Army Headquarters for Europe. The hospital was a VIP hospital and the dental clinic was excellent. The headquarters and hospital had excellent connections, which provided top quality care for the people at the hospital.

I phoned Pearl, who was very pleased because her parents were in Switzerland at that time. My orders were to go to McGuire Air Force Base in New Jersey and fly to Germany on a military plane. The only downside was that Pearl and the kids had to stay in Salt Lake longer than originally planned.

After a few days leave in Salt Lake, I flew to Washington D. C. and visited Jay and Gloria Nichols for a couple of days. They were very good to take me sightseeing, as I had never been to that area. Jay drove me to McGuire air base in New Jersey where I boarded a MATS C118 (I think that was the plane designation). It was the military version of a civilian DC-7 and was a four motor propeller plane. We stopped in Newfoundland to refuel, and then went to the Azore Islands to refuel again. We took off from the Azores for Frankfurt, Germany. When we were about 1 hour into the flight, one of the motors quit running. I was looking out the window and watched as the propeller on the number three engine slowed down, then sped up, and then belch flames for a few moments. The pilot turned the engine off and feathered the propeller. He then announced on the intercom that we would have to return to the Azores and that a rescue plane was already on its way just in case of an emergency arose. He said there was nothing to worry about because the plane could fly on three engines very well.

About fifteen minutes later, I could see the number two engine acting up similar to the engine that had just gone out. For the first time in my life, I wondered if we were going to have to ditch the plane in the ocean, and what that would be like. Fortunately, the engine kept running, and we made it back to the Azores.

Eight hours of repairs didn't work out as planned, so we were unloaded a second time just before we were to take off. Finally after twelve hours, we were loaded onto a different plane, a Lockheed Constellation, and took off for Germany. That flight went smoothly.

During the flight, the pilot was nice enough to invite anyone interested to walk to the front of the plane and look at the cockpit. When my turn came, it was a moment I will never forget. The time was about four a.m. and the white puffy clouds cleared just as we approached Paris, France. I could see the Eiffel Tower, the Arc of Triumph, and the city was lit up like a picture post card. My first look at Europe was really spectacular. The airplane's altitude was low enough so that the landmarks were easy to view. Today's jet aircraft fly so high this type of view would be impossible.

We landed at the air base in Frankfurt and everyone was taken to the train station to catch a modern electric train to their new assignments. I meet Bill Neale at that time. We had been at Ft. Sam and on the same plane but had never met. We rode the train to Heidelberg and were met by our commanding officer, Colonel Clair Budge. He was very nice and got us situated at the BOQ and the hospital. BOQ stands for Bachelor Officer Quarters.

I took an advance on my salary and bought an 1955 used Volkswagen bug for $700.00. That was the second time I had ever borrowed money to buy anything.

I stayed in the BOQ until Pearl, Mark, and Sue arrived in October. We decided to pay for Pearl to fly to Switzerland. The Army usually provided transportation for Officer's dependents; however, a new regulation mandated that unless one would spend three years overseas, the Army would not pay transportation costs for dependents. My obligation was for two years.

Pearl and the children flew to Zurich, Switzerland via commercial airline in October 1957. One of the hospital dentists, Grady King, had been to Switzerland a few times. He said he would go with me to meet the plane. He could speak pretty good German. I asked him if we needed a map or anything. I was not familiar driving in Europe and we would have to leave at two a.m. to meet the plane. Grady said we didn't need anything because he had driven to Switzerland and was familiar with the route.

When I picked him up at two in the morning, I discovered he had been out partying and was drunk. I was upset because I would now have to go alone and without a map. It was a dark rainy night, and the Autobahn only went half way to my destination. I was new in Germany and had never driven outside Heidelberg. It was necessary to drive on secondary narrow roads, which weren't marked very well. It was an unpleasant experience to drive in two foreign countries at night and go through Customs at the border where special papers are needed.

I finally made it to the airport thirty minutes early. After parking, I walked around when all of the sudden, I saw Pearl and the kids. Mark

119

and Sue were playing on the grass outside the airport. It was a wonderful reunion. Pearl's plane had arrived one hour early. Pearl's parents showed up shortly after I got there. We drove one hour to the temple and the lovely temple home where the Trauffers lived. Pearl and the children stayed with the Traffers, as they hadn't seen each other for several months.

I stayed two days and drove back to base alone on Sunday. I was unfamiliar with the border city Basel, and got onto a one-way street headed into to France, rather than Germany. The French border guards wouldn't let me proceed because I didn't have the proper papers. They acted as if they didn't understand English. After thirty minutes, they allowed me to turn around and go back to the Basel, Switzerland. I finally made it to the German border and returned to Heidelberg. It was another very dark, rainy night. The two-lane road was very narrow with lots of hills and curves and a great number of slow moving trucks.

The work at the dental clinic was very pleasant. We had good facilities and equipment. Appointments were one-hour long and you weren't pushed to do poor quality work and lots of it. There were eight American Army dentists and eight German civilian dentists. There was a nice, big dental laboratory with eight German dental lab technicians. The lab did work for several small outlying dental clinics. We worked on dependents as well as military personal. There were many high-ranking military officers and American civilians who worked for the Department of the Army. Twenty-two generals were stationed in Heidelberg and ninety bird colonels. Once in a while we would have a patient from a NATO country.

Occasionally I worked on a General's wife. The high-ranking people were always very nice. There wasn't much military protocol in the hospital, especially where the doctors were concerned.

I was given a NATO assignment that I never told Pearl about, at the time. If a war started, I would be the closest dentist to the war zone, nine miles from the border. We practiced outdoor exercises once a month in a field hospital tent. I didn't want Pearl to worry about a war.

There was a servicemen's branch of the LDS Church in Heidelberg. The leader was a young man named Lynn Bracken, who was a chair side assistant at the dental clinic. He knew I was coming and was LDS. I went to church before Pearl arrived and liked all of the young soldiers who attended the meetings. I was always the only officer who was active in church. After a few months, Lynn Bracken rotated back to the states, so I was asked to be the Servicemen's Group Leader. A year later a Servicemen's Branch was created. We had a lovely chapel, which was the first LDS Church building built in West Germany after the war. There was also a German branch that met in the same building. Theodore S. Burton was the mission president and we got to know him and his family pretty well. Each year we were able to go to a religious retreat in Berchtesgaden in Bavaria. That was a real treat because Pearl's parents were always there.

We saw American Mormons from all around Europe. Often we knew someone, or knew of someone from back in the States. There was always a lot to talk about and much excitement to be around a large number of the Saints. We made some wonderful friends from the branch. I was the branch president until we left in August 1960. The first leadership positions I had in the church were as the group leader and branch President, which were very rewarding.

Once I knew exactly when Pearl and the kids would be In Germany, I embarked on a search to find us a place to stay. There was a shortage of apartments, but I found a small apartment in Ziegelhausen, a small town along the Nekkar River. It was eight kilometers from the hospital. I drove the six hours to Switzerland, and picked up Pearl and the kids. We set up our household in Ziegelhausen, Germany. We were very happy and things were good.

The apartment did not have central heating and was not well insulated. It was windy and cold. At night after the kids were in bed, Pearl and I would sit in the small kitchen by the stove to read. After a few minutes we would turn around so we could warm our cold side, which was to face away from the stove. The stove didn't put out very much heat because charcoal briquettes burned longer but with less heat than coal. The stove was our only means of heat. The kids had heavy pajamas, and we would usually go to bed early to stay warm.

We spent Christmas 1957 with Pearl's Family in Switzerland. Several Swiss missionaries were invited to President Trauffer's home on Christmas Eve. We had a nice party. That was the first time we met a missionary named Lee Barnes, who eventually married Pearl's youngest sister Evelyn.

It was very nice to be out of school and earning money. The exchange rate of dollars to Deutsch marks was 4.2 marks to the dollar. This greatly increased our buying power. In addition, the PX commissary, with no sales tax, along with military gas at 15 cents a gallon, made us financially well off.

Fred Distlehorst

The Army mixed up our hold baggage in Ft. Douglas, Utah, which delayed its arrival for four months. After straightening out the mix up, our six hundred pounds of luggage, which had the kids' winter clothing in it, arrived in January. On February 1, 1958, a dentist friend named Fred Distlehorst and I left to go skiing at Kitzbuhel, Austria. I had always had a great desire to become a good skier. I was able to go a few times in high school and a few times while attending the University of Wyoming. I never advanced much beyond a beginner skier. I was finally able to buy nice equipment and take up the sport in a serious way.

Fred had just bought a new 1957 Mercedes 190 SL sports car. Believe it or not, the price was $3,750.00. That price was one of the good things about the "good old days." The two of us left Friday after work to go skiing in Austria. Fred didn't feel well, so he asked me to drive. It was the first time I had ever driven a sports car, and it was fun. I drove to Munich. When we got to the border, Fred felt well enough after sleeping in the car, so he took over the driving. I moved to the passenger side, buckled up the seat belt, and went to sleep. I awoke once and thought of unbuckling the seat belt because it was a little confining but decided not to because we were in a blizzard. I liked the idea of seat belts. I believe I had some divine help with that decision to stay buckled up.

That was the first model car that had seat belts (the first seat belts were lap belts without the shoulder strap). That decision saved my life. The next time I awoke, I could feel the car was fish tailing and out of control. I opened my eyes and looked to see the road curved ahead and that we were going off the road and down the mountain. The headlights were like search lights pointed straight out into the darkness and then they dropped down. It looked as if we were going off a cliff.

A quick thought went through my mind: *How far down before we crash?* It turned out that the drop off wasn't a big cliff. Nevertheless, we summersaulted down the mountain. When we stopped, the car was upside down. One minute we were warm and comfortable in the car listening to the radio, and the next minute my life had changed forever.

Heidelberg Military Housing Our VW in Front of our Apartment

After the car came to a halt, I tried to unbuckle my seat belt and realized my right arm was broken. I asked Fred if he was okay, and he said yes. He asked if I was okay, and I told him I thought my arm was broken but other than that I was okay. The roof of the sports car was smashed down, so the passenger space was very small. I was suspended upside down but was able to unbuckle the seat belt and twist so that I was on lying on my back. I tried to get out of the car but found I couldn't. The door was jammed closed and there wasn't any window room as the roof had been pushed down. Fred was a small guy and was able to squeeze out through the window space on his side of the car. He got wet because the car came to rest in a half frozen stream at the bottom of the hill. I couldn't get over to his side because of the bent roof so I was trapped inside the car.

Fred didn't say a word – just took off. I could hear the squeak of his boots in the snow. I thought he would try to get me out or at least say something. I was so surprised I didn't say anything before he got out of hearing range. I knew Fred would go for help. We were lucky Fred could exit the car because we were quite a distance off the road at the bottom of a hill. Snow and darkness hid the car.

My next thought was that if the water from the stream came into the car, I would be in real trouble. It was a stormy cold February night. I was in the mountains in a very remote area of Austria. Hypothermia could be fatal. I felt that it would take at least two hours to get help and maybe longer at one a.m. in the morning.

Fortunately, the water didn't come on my side of the car. It was the darkest and loneliest time of my life.

In about fifteen minutes, I heard voices and found out later that Fred had climbed up to the road and was able to stop a group of cars that had been to a tavern for a party. In Europe, most people didn't have large homes, so they would rent a tavern for parties. Fred was very cold, wet, and had gone to get help. He didn't think I could get out of the car without the help of a wrecker truck. We were lucky on a stormy night, in a remote area, at that time of the night, to have a group of cars come along. One man in the group was a legitimate Prince, from Austria and Madam Renault of the Renault Car Company (the biggest in France) was another member of the party group. It was a very distinguished group of people that gave me help.

The Prince was in charge, came down to the car, spoke in English, and asked if I was okay. I told him about the broken arm and that I was okay. He told me not to worry, that they would have me out of the car shortly, that I would live many more years and have many children. That sounded really good to me.

The group of four or five men tried to upright the car at first. When they found out that they couldn't do that, they dragged the car away from the water. The Prince then sent one man back to the cars to get a jack handle. They spoke German, so I didn't know exactly what was said. The Prince then proceeded to pry the door open. They soon helped me out of the car and I thanked them from the bottom of my heart.

We walked up to the road and looked back to see the beautiful sports car upside down. I found that as long as I kept my arm supported in my belt, the arm didn't hurt very much. I was driven to the nearest town, which was St. Joseph, Austria by two Austrian men. When we reached the town, the driver turned on the wrong road into a cemetery rather than the hospital and we had a good laugh.

We couldn't speak much due to the language differences. At the hospital, a doctor was called in and X-rays were taken. The doctor told me in broken English that it was a very bad break, that he would set the bones, and put a cast on my arm. A nurse dripped some anesthetic on a cloth placed over my nose, and I was put out quickly.

An Autobiography

When I awoke a few hours later, a nurse who was wearing a very large white hat, was sitting on a chair next the bed. She didn't speak English, and I didn't speak German but I signaled to her I had to throw up. I discovered at that time that I had a bleeding bruise on my left cheek. She gave me a pan, I did my thing, and went back to sleep.

The next time I awoke, it was early morning, and I was cold. The nurse was gone and had taken the hot water bottle that had been on my feet. The nice down filled comforters were always too short in Europe. Fred came with his girlfriend and said they would be back in a few hours when I could be released from the hospital. After I was released, Fred asked me if I wanted to stay in Kitzbuhel or go back to Heidelberg. I told him I wanted to go back to the hospital in Heidelberg as soon as possible. We took the first available train and got back to Heidelberg

Saturday, at about nine p.m., my arm started to swell while I rode on the train, even though I had it elevated. That swelling inside the hard plaster cast caused me a great deal of pain. I was afraid that the circulation might be cut off to my arm, which could cause nerve damage or even the loss of the arm. It was a long painful ride back to Heidelberg.

After we got back to the hospital, a sergeant I knew cut the cast off. It was a great relief to ease the pain, even though the hair on my arm stuck to the plaster. No wrap was put between my arm and the plaster. The next morning, which was Sunday, I phoned Pearl and kidded her a little then told her about the accident and broken arm. She didn't believe it at first because she thought I was joking. After church, she came to see me.

On Monday, Colonel Budge told me that the best orthopedic Army doctor was in Frankfurt and that I would be sent there. He also asked me if I wanted to be sent back to the USA. I told him I wanted to stay in Germany. The normal evacuation channel would have been to send me to a general hospital in Landstuhl, Germany. Army regulations called for a soldier to be evacuated back to the States if he would be away from duty for ninety days. It was nice to have Colonel Budge in a position to help me.

I was taken to Frankfurt by ambulance. X-rays showed the radius bone had two breaks and the ulna bone had one. Surgery was performed. The head of the radius bone was removed because it had such a poor blood supply that it would have left me with a stiff arm. A pin was put in the ulna bone, which protruded one inch outside of the skin at the elbow.

The next day I complained of wrist pain and another x-ray was taken. The second x-ray showed the bones had separated along the pin. The doctor told me another operation was needed to get the two ends of the bone to touch, but the bone chips that had been taken from my hip could still be used. He was a good surgeon and also said that if anything ever went wrong, it almost always happened with a person who worked in the medical field.

Earlier I had gotten out of bed to empty my bladder and discovered my right leg felt like rubber, and was weak. The reason was because of the bone chips that had been taken from the ileum area of the pelvic bone to aid healing. Nothing was ever mentioned to me about the bone chips prior to surgery.

The second operation was scheduled to be performed under local anesthesia. I was given a shot with a long needle that went from my clavicle to my armpit. As I was lying on the operating table, my arm was resting on my stomach, and the arm got numb. I couldn't move the arm because the nerves to the muscles were also anesthetized. I watched as my arm slowly fell from my chest and wound up hanging to the side of the table. It was a terrible experience to not be able to move my arm and thinking it would hurt if it dangled down. I was relieved it didn't hurt but it was still an unpleasant experience. It gave me some insight into what it would be like to have some part of the body paralyzed.

The doctor decided general anesthesia was needed and the second operation went fine. I was kept in the hospital in Frankfurt for eight weeks and then released. The cast on my arm remained for five and one half months. The pin that protruded from my elbow was removed after six months. In those days, physical therapists did not exist. The doctor made a tomahawk for me and showed me how to use it to gain more motion.

When the cast was removed, my arm was very small due to no muscle movement for more than five months. The skin looked bad too. The elbow joint hardly moved to bend or extend my arm. Twisting motions, pronation, and supination were also very restricted. I worked many hours and eventually, the motion increased to where a point where the doctor thought it was an excellent outcome. I think I have about 80% of the normal joint strength and motion. If I put too much stress on the elbow it hurts.

Missing an inch of bone left a weak elbow joint. The wrist had also been affected. Given the severity of the problem, the result was very good. One learns to live with things like that. I am grateful for the wonderful treatment I received. Nowadays, surgical procedures have been improved.

While the cast was still in place, I had cut a small hole in the plaster cast with a dental drill and used a metal coat hanger to gain relief from the itchiness.

As soon as I got out of the hospital, I drove to Switzerland to be with the family. While driving around Bern with the family, a construction truck tire threw a rock that came through the windshield of our VW and hit me in the chest. Fortunately, I was driving slowly in the city and no one was hurt. It made a six inch round hole in the windshield.

After a few days in Switzerland, I returned to my hospital and went to work. I did prosthetics with the cast on my arm until the cast was removed. I handled a full load of work. When my first commanding officer (C.O.) was transferred and a new colonel took over, the new C.O. decided I should take his place and be the prosthetic officer for the clinic. This turned out to be a wonderful assignment and gave me valuable experience, which helped in orthodontics. Usually a career dental specialist (Prosthodontist) was given the assignment in a V.I.P hospital. Eventually, I was also made the supply officer for the dental clinic. I think I got that job because I was easy going. I was nervous to be responsible for all the equipment and supplies. If something big went wrong, I was responsible. Fortunately, I had a very good and experienced sergeant who did most of the work. I greatly enjoyed the work at the dental clinic and my association with the American and German physicians and dentists.

The last working day at the hospital before I would be transferred back to the USA, I was told to report to the hospital commander's office. I was very surprised to be presented with an award during a brief ceremony. The award was a Certificate of Achievement. Only two awards were given in a group of over 300 dentists in Europe that year. It was a nice honor usually given to a career officer.

First Orthodontic Training

Trauffers & Swiss Temple Home

About halfway through my tour of duty in Germany, I went to the University of Heidelberg to look at their orthodontic department to see how they did things and what I could learn. I could not speak the language. The University people were nice to me and referred me to Dr. Hans Kaufman, who was a practicing orthodontist. Dr. Kaufman spoke very good English and treated several American children. His father had been on the facility of the dental school at the university.

Dr. Kaufman had a very interesting World War II history. He lost an eye while fighting on the Eastern Front against the Russians when he was eighteen years old. We became good friends and I went to his office on many Saturdays to observe and learn. He found a German orthodontic textbook that had been translated into English. The German treatment methods for orthodontics were very different from that used in the U. S. Eventually, I treated about fifteen patients under Dr. Kaufman's direction. I learned a lot about removable orthodontic appliances, which was the main European approach to orthodontics. The American approach was almost entirely fixed appliances (braces attached to each tooth).

129

Gus G. Angelos

Since that time, most European schools have changed their practices and teach fixed appliances. The problem at that time was the economics, along with socialized medicine, and dentistry in European countries. The German national insurance had a certain amount of money budgeted for orthodontics. A great many more patients could be treated with removable appliances. The results were not as good as the American way with fixed appliances. Nevertheless, more patients benefitted from treatment. The fixed appliances allowed more control over the teeth. The knowledge and experience I gained in Heidelberg helped me when I became an orthodontist.

During the time I was observing and helping Dr. Kaufman, one American patient's mother asked if I could see her daughter for appointments at the hospital because they lived in military housing close to the hospital, and it would be more convenient. Dr. Kaufman's office was across the river and a few miles away. Dr. Kaufman said it was okay and so I saw the patient a few times for short appointments at the hospital.

One day as I was working on a military patient, one of the dentists who had finished early with an appointment, walked in to say he would finish the work on my patient, as the colonel wanted to see me immediately in his office. This was very unusual. I reported to the colonel who told me that a major had filed a report to claim that I was treating his daughter at the hospital for money. This accusation was a very serious violation of Army regulations. I told the colonel the whole story. The colonel knew I didn't take coffee breaks and that I had seen the patient on my own time. Dr. Kaufman received the money for the treatment. I never received any money from Dr. Kaufman or anyone. I only wanted to further my knowledge about orthodontics.

The colonel liked me and told me I was the biggest producer of dentistry in the clinic. I was surprised to hear I had done more work than the other dentists. The colonel understood that I was doing the people a favor and didn't have a private practice on the side. A big deal was made of it. The hospital brass were offended that one of their doctors (me) would be accused of dishonesty while trying to help someone. The German orthodontist was very offended and threw the treatment fee on the steps of the major's quarters and refused to continue treatment on the major's daughter.

130

An Autobiography

It was very important to keep good relations between the German people and the American military. This was an important United States policy during the Cold War. In the end, the major got into hot water, instead of me. I always practiced dentistry the way I was taught in school. Do it right, and do it to the best of your ability.

Shortly after I arrived, I did a favor for a career sergeant and finished a fixed bridge that an American dentist had really dragged on for months, with him refusing to complete it. Two years later, one of the German chair-side assistants told me that she had assisted many American dentists over a period of ten years. She had noticed the work habits, ethics, and type of work the American dentists did over the years. She said that the first time she assisted me, she knew I was a very good dentist who did things right. It never occurred to me that the dentists would be talked about and earn a reputation among the many German hospital employees.

The military hospital was half-staffed by American Army personal and half-staffed by German civilian employees. I was always happy to go the extra mile for the men in the Army who were making the military their career. On one occasion, I made some dentures in a real hurry for a sergeant who didn't have any teeth. He had refused treatment as he was eating okay. Suddenly he needed to return to the U. S. for a family emergency. He was concerned about seeing all his family members, and without teeth. The colonel told the sergeant there wasn't enough time to do the work before the sergeant had to leave. It wasn't a big deal, so I made the dentures. The sergeant was very grateful and asked me if I wanted any sleeping bags or military equipment for camping or items like that. He was in supply and could get items, I think in a dishonest way. I told him "no thanks." He then asked if I had applied for available space on a military ship that cruised around the Mediterranean Sea. This ship dropped off military people at their new duty stations and was the best bargain in Europe, as you only paid for your meals which amounted to about $5.00 a day. It was very difficult to go on the cruise because of politics and military regulations. It was a dream of mine before cruise ships became popular for vacations.

The sergeant said his buddy in Italy was the one who made the arrangements for those who applied to go on the cruise. The usual application took about three years to process and would be put on a list. Often in Heidelberg, only the high-ranking officers were successful with getting on the military ships. I had applied but didn't think it would ever come to pass.

That afternoon the sergeant phoned me for some passport information and said it was all set and that Pearl and I would be accepted in one year. I didn't believe it, but it actually happened. Pearl and I sailed on a military ship from Italy around the Mediterranean Sea to Greece and Turkey the following year.

Pearl and I had many wonderful vacations around Europe. What made it even nicer was the fact we could take our children to Switzerland, and Grandpa and Grandma Trauffer would tend them with great love and care. All but two of the Trauffer's fifteen grandchildren were born while they were away at the Swiss Temple. They were always thrilled to see Mark and Sue and baby Scott.

We traveled to most all the Countries of Western Europe and Scandinavia. Sometimes we went with friends and sometimes alone. We usually drove our VW bug and could buy gas at the military base for fifteen cents a gallon. Sometimes we camped out.

We went to the 1958 World's Fair in Brussels, Belgium and camped out. It was very interesting and a great adventure to see so much of Europe. On the Mediterranean Cruse, the ship stopped at Athens, Greece the third day out. My cousin George and his wife Maria Nicholopolos met us at the ship and showed us around. They treated us like royalty. It was thrilling to see the country where my Father was born and raised.

We went to East Berlin in 1959 just before the Berlin Wall was erected. We went to the city where my mother was born. We met all of Pearl's relatives in Switzerland and saw all the areas where her parents had lived and traveled prior to immigrating to America. The three years in Europe were a wonderful time in our life. It was like a three-year dream vacation.

The beautiful Temple home that the Trauffers lived in was always open to us and Grandma and Grandpa Trauffer were the best baby sitters anyone could ask for. They were always happy to tend our children when we wanted to travel. The Trauffers had a constant group of church people coming and going. One time when we were staying there for a few days, Elder Hugh B. Brown, an Apostle, who later become a member of the First Presidency, and his daughter were houseguests. Very early Sunday morning Pearl and I were awakened and I was asked to drive Walt and Elder Brown to Geneva, which was about two hours away. The temple car had a flat tire. The two men needed to be at meetings and were in great need of a car for the day. They didn't want to borrow my car and I was very happy to be their driver. The two men were tall and had to squeeze into my VW Beetle. They were good sports and we made it just fine. I had a chance to visit most of the day with Elder Brown, who was in the front seat. It was a wonderful experience for a whole day to be in the presence of two such great men doing church business.

The biggest and best event while we were in Germany was the birth of Scott on May 30, 1959. As I hadn't been present when Mark and Sue were born, so I looked forward to being at the hospital when Scott was born. As it turned out, our babysitter was a lovely grandma from the branch but she got sick during the day Scott was born. I had no choice but to stay home to take care of Mark and Sue … and the baby sitter. The hospital staff was supposed to phone me when Pearl went into labor. They forgot to phone and when I phoned to see how Pearl was doing, I was told that Scott had been born. Scott was our biggest baby and fit into our family very well. One of Pearl's many strong

Scott George Angelos

133

points was being a great mother and taking great care of our children. She always knew where they were and what they were doing. I can't tell you how much joy and happiness they brought to us as parents. We took about a thousand 35-millimeter slides and photos in Europe. They are old and outdated, but we love them. We have scanned many into our computer.

During December 1959, my Father became very ill and the doctor was not sure if he would live. I traveled to Salt Lake City on an emergency leave. My dad made it through that time. While in Salt Lake, I was able to attend Lee Barnes and Evelyn Trauffer's wedding in the Salt Lake Temple. Pearl's mom came home for the wedding but her father had to stay at the Temple.

After three years in Germany, I was once again asked what area I would like to be assigned to. I requested Utah or California. The Army had four Dentists in Utah. Two stationed at Dugway, Utah and two at Fort Douglas in Salt Lake. I lucked out and was assigned to Dugway. While in Germany, I applied to go to five dental schools that had postgraduate orthodontic programs. I was not accepted to any of them. An applicant pretty much had to be in the top 10% of their dental school class academically to get accepted into an orthodontic program. I ended up 52nd in a class of 103 as I wrote earlier. I had hoped that other factors might help me get accepted, but it didn't happen. I believe that grades account for 90% of acceptance consideration. The only other way I could become a bonafide orthodontic specialist was through a preceptorship program that the American Dental Association (ADA) and American Association of Orthodontist, (AAO) had. This program had been in effect for about ten years due to the shortage of orthodontists and limited schools programs. I was not ready to separate from the service because I only had a California license and wasn't sure I wanted to be a general dentist and practice in California. I still had a strong desire to specialize. I could have left the service and started a practice in California but chose not to do that.

In the 1960's California presented a great opportunity for dentists to start a practice and do well financially. It has always been legal for a dentist to do orthodontic work on patients. One should have specialty training to do good work otherwise one would not be considered a real specialist and could not represent yourself as such. In order to be recognized and a fully qualified specialist, it was necessary to complete a postgraduate program recognized by the American Dental Association. I wanted to be an orthodontist because I thought I would enjoy that type of practice more than being a general practitioner. Income was never the issue. I felt I could be happy and make a good living as a general dentist. Additional training would only delay my desire to settle down. I decided to go for it and Pearl agreed.

Upon completing my assignment in Germany, our family flew together back to McGuire Air Base. We went to Jersey City the first night back in the good old USA. The next morning I went to the dock in New York City to pick up our newly purchased used Rambler Station Wagon only to find that the battery had been stolen. It was scary to be in that area of New York, even in the daylight. I eventually found a new battery, picked up Pearl and the kids, and we started driving to the Nichols' home in Nebraska. We had lots of car troubles with that car. We had a wonderful time traveling with the Nichols to Salt Lake. It has always been a lot of fun to be around our family.

Gus G. Angelos

Dugway

I reported to Dugway and started to work at the small base hospital. There were two dentists stationed there for the military people, although we provided emergency work on civilians because of the isolated location. The other dentist was Lt. Col. Charles Yates who was a wonderful southern gentleman. He was deferred from military service during W.W. II but was drafted into the Army during the Korean War and in the Army, found a home. He was a real good buddy of the base commander Col Armitage. They were both southern boys who owned horses and often rode together.

Dugway had wild mustang horses all around the housing area because the base commander liked horses and allowed them free access to the housing area. The horses just did what they wanted to. You could get close to them, and even feed grass to a few, but they could take care of themselves. All the medical doctors at the hospital were young and were in the service for two years. There was an LDS ward on the base and many civilians who lived on the base were LDS.

Dugway's mission was to develop and test chemical, biological, and radiological weapons. Most of the base area was restricted unless one had a top security clearance. The housing area was open to almost anyone after showing a drivers license to the military police at the gate.

We had a nice house and lived a very good family life. The base had a nice gym, a swimming pool, and recreation facilities. We were also close enough to Salt Lake to visit our families. It was eighty-six miles to Salt Lake City. Our ward had quite a few young families with children and many wonderful people there. Nearly all of the ward members were civilians. I was the only active officer in the ward.

The only downside to the assignment was the dentist I worked with. He was the most incompetent dentist you can imagine. Because of so many complaints and problems, the Eighth Army sent a special investigator from California to Dugway to check on him. The outcome of this was that word was sent to the next duty station that Lt. Col. Yates should not do dental work on patients, only exams. The Army even sent him to Korea, which was a very undesirable assignment. A Sargent who knew someone else in Korea told this information to me. I am not sure if this was true.

From the start, the hospital staff wanted to see me for their dental work and not the colonel. It took me a while to catch on. When Col. Yates was away, even the hospital commander, a M. D., would pop in and ooze all his charm to ask me to work in his family for dental work. As the hospital commander, it was very awkward to make appointments to bypass Col. Yates in order to see me, the captain. There were some lawsuits filed against Col. Yates for malpractice, as well as numerous complaints from military people. With one patient, the colonel had replaced the same filling twenty-three times because it kept falling out. I did it once, which still held some ten years later when I saw the patient. Fortunately for me, I knew the investigating officer the Army had sent from California. When I showed him x-rays of Colonel Yates' work he couldn't believe it.

Colonel Yates was always nice to me. I found out from the commanding officer's Sergeant Major that Colonel Yates wrote a mediocre efficiency report on me. Efficiency reports were the means by which officers were evaluated and which were very important for promotions in the Army. They were written every year by your commanding officer and then reviewed by his commanding officer. The hospital commander forced Colonel Yates change my report. The Sergeant Major of the hospital told me this in private.

I was promoted to major just prior to separating from the army in July 1962. Had I stayed in the Army another month, I would have pinned on the insignia in September and officially been a Major. It was only a matter of time as the promotion was official and complete.

I have many pleasant memories of our years at Dugway. In September, when our new Volkswagen bug arrived in Oakland, California,

An Autobiography

I was notified. The price of the car was $1,172.00 in Germany. The price in the U.S. was $1800. I had done dental work on an army pilot stationed at Dugway and asked him to let me know if he anticipated a flight to California within the next few weeks. The pilot phoned at just the right time and said he was flying alone to San Francisco to pick up a general. I was able to fly with him in a two motor airplane to a small landing strip right by the Golden Gate Bridge. We arrived at four p.m. on a Friday and the bridges around San Francisco were extremely crowded with people leaving San Francisco for the weekend. I was in an isolated area without a car and needed to get across the bay to Oakland Army Terminal quickly. I went to the base operation shack and asked the man there if he could help me. Luckily a National Guard helicopter pilot was practicing take offs and landings. I was able to hitch a ride in the helicopter across the Bay to the Oakland Army Terminal.

Along the way I saw Fisherman's Wharf and lots of nice sights from a low altitude. When we got to the Oakland Army Terminal, the military police drove out to see the V.I.P. who rated a helicopter. It wasn't a V.I.P., only me, but they were nice enough to take me to the right place to pick up my new car. That was one time in my life I saw what it was like to have a private plane and helicopter at my service. I was extremely lucky because it was a big base and I didn't know where to go. I got the car just before closing on Friday. That connection saved me two days. It also allowed me to drive to Fairfield and spend some time talking to Dr. Joel Gillespie about the possibility of a preceptorship and still get home two days early.

Another fun experience I had was playing on the ward basketball and softball teams. We took second place in the All-Church Slow Pitch Softball tournament when slow pitch was first gaining popularity. Once when the Harlem Globetrotters basketball team came to Salt Lake City, the ward team played their accompanying farm team called the Harlem Clowns. The Dugway Base basketball team was scheduled to play the Clowns, however something happened and the Base team couldn't play the game. I received a last minute phone call to ask if our ward basketball team could play. We did and it was a lot of fun and a very special experience. They even charged money to see the game. That doesn't happen to many ward basketball teams.

Four months after my return to America, on December 8, 1960, my Dad died. He and mother had stayed in Salt Lake until November to vote for John F. Kennedy for president. Then they drove to Las Vegas to spend time with Uncle Nick. The warmer climate and lower elevation helped dad. Dad was not in good health the last few years of his life. He died when he was 67 years old. He always seemed old to me. I really felt bad that he worked so long and hard, without any hobbies or interests other than work and the family.

He always had wanted to go back to Greece to see his family. When I was stationed in Germany, I invited my parents to visit us, rest, and then go to Greece. I offered to pay for the tickets, but dad's health wouldn't allow it. He was a good man and I loved him dearly.

When dad passed away, mother phoned Sam, who phoned me at Dugway. We took a train to Las Vegas. As soon as we walked in the door, mother went to the bedroom and got dad's diamond ring, which she gave to me. Dad wanted me to have it. Sam had a diamond ring he received from our parents as a high school graduation present. When I graduated from high school, mom asked me what I wanted as a gift. I asked for and received a nice portable radio. Portable radios were new in those days, not like the inexpensive battery radios of today. I never cared for any kind of jewelry and have never worn any except a watch. I appreciated the sentiment of dad's ring, but thought it would be better for Sam to have because he would wear it. Several years later I gave the ring to Sam. He always liked jewelry. There was a misunderstanding about one of mother's diamond rings. Apparently Mother told Margaret and Sam's wife, Joy, at different times that a certain diamond ring would go to them when mom died. Joy wound up with the ring and Margaret's feelings were hurt because the ring belonged to our grandmother. I didn't find out about this for several years. I gave dad's ring to Sam, and then Joy gave mother's ring to Margaret, which was nice. I think mother always intended for Margaret to have that ring, but mom became forgetful toward the end of her life. I felt that Margaret deserved the ring because it originally had come from mother's mother. Margaret was always very close to mom and took excellent care of her, especially during the last few years of mom's life when she lived with Margaret.

Dad's funeral was held in the Greek Orthodox Church in Salt Lake City on December 10, 1960. On December 9, my grandmother (mom's mother) was killed in an auto accident near St. George, Utah. She and her husband were driving to Salt Lake to attend dad's funeral. It was extremely hard on my mother to loose both her husband and mother in one week. Mother had seen dad get ill and always be able to recover. I don't think she was prepared for him to die. I tried to tell mom that he could go anytime, but she was in denial.

I had taken dad to two doctors and talked to them about dad's health problems and knew he was very ill. He died from congestive heart failure and arteriosclerosis and arthrosclerosis (hardening of the arteries and plaque build up inside the arteries). It took mom over a year to get over the loss of her two closest loved ones, not including her children.

The best thing that happened at Dugway was the birth of our last child, Craig. Everything went well with the pregnancy and delivery. I was even able to be present during the delivery. This wasn't allowed in civilian hospitals in those days, but the military situation at Dugway made it possible for me. The birth of a baby is a real miracle. It is especially meaningful when it is your own child, the baby is normal, and mom comes through in good shape. Seeing the birth of Craig is one of my all-time great experiences. It is a real miracle to see the birth of one of God's children. I was also happy to finally be there for the birth of one of our children from start to finish.

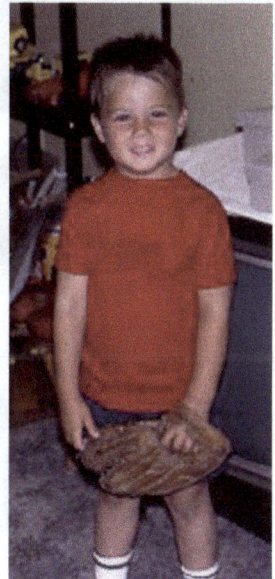

Craig Walter Angelos

We also acquired our first family dog, Diamond, while at Dugway. Diamond was half English Pointer and half Springer Spaniel. She was six weeks old when we got her from a friend. Diamond had a white diamond patch on her forehead. Mark and Sue picked her out, and Mark named her. She turned out to be a wonderful family member for sixteen years. More will be written about the dog later.

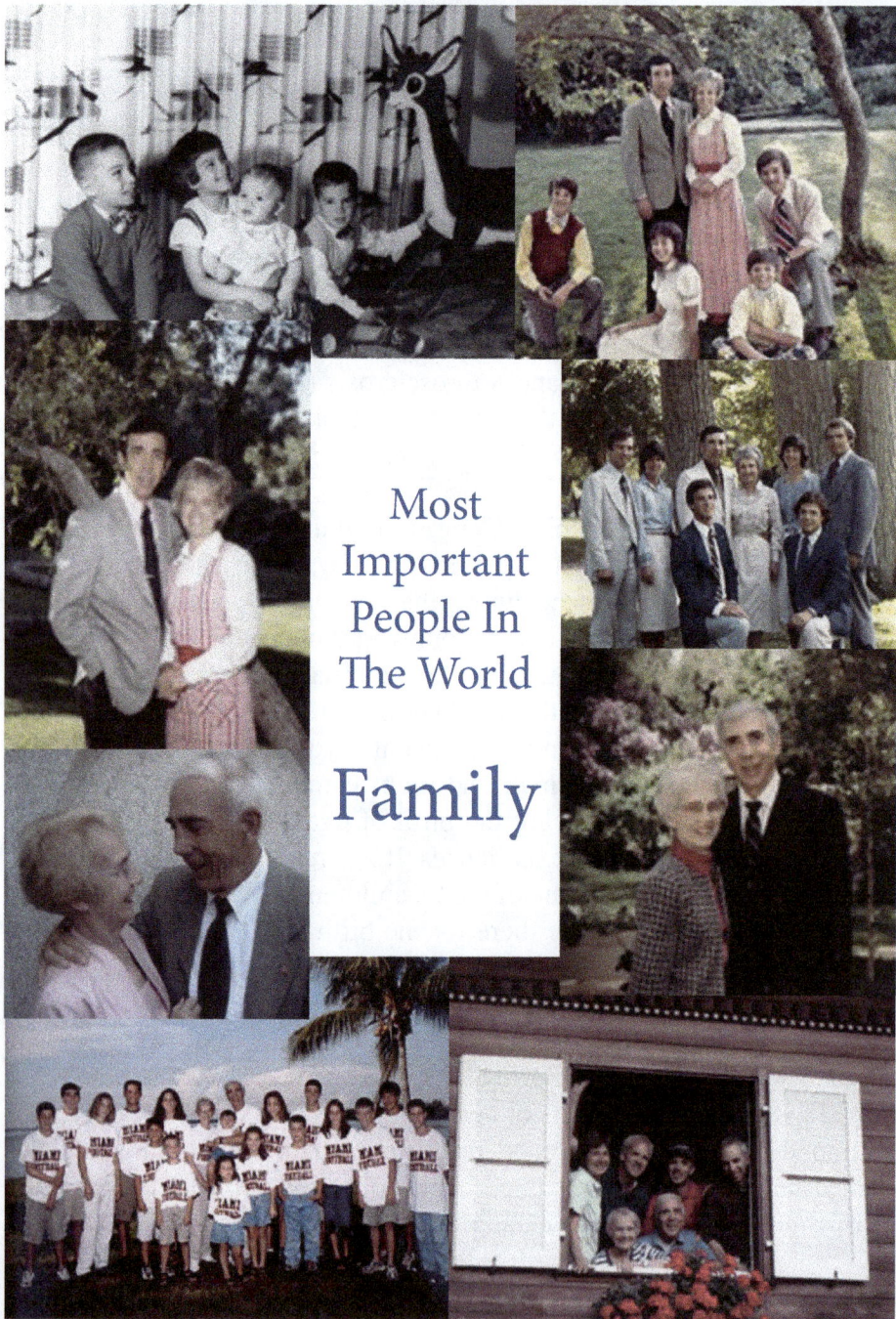

Most
Important
People In
The World

Family

An Autobiography

While stationed at Dugway, I was able to take the Wyoming and Utah State Dental Board Exams. I received licenses to practice in both those states. Each one of those board exams were given at the state prison, under difficult conditions. The state furnished only a card table, a canvas director's chair, electrical outlets, and the patients – who were convicts. During the Utah exam, there was a prison break, which really caused excitement. Utah also required a new basic science exam in addition to the regular written dental exam. I was six years out of school and was among only eight of the sixty-five dentists to pass all six sections of the new exam on the first try.

At Wyoming, I was the only non-resident who passed the board exam. There were six men from out of state plus nine residents who took the Wyoming exam. I think having gone to the University of Wyoming was very helpful. Life can be interesting and very political at times.

I put in the necessary papers to separate from the Army and was turned down because of a Berlin Crisis between the Soviet Union and the USA. The following year, I again submitted the necessary papers to separate from the army. The world situation had calmed down and I was able to leave the Army having served five years and two days active duty. While still in the Army, I applied for an Army program, which would have sent me to Kansas City's dental school for two years to become an orthodontist. A colonel at the Pentagon told me that the arrangement at Kansas City had not been finalized and that I would probably be chosen the following year. In the mean time, if I wanted to specialize in another area, the Army would probably approve it and send me to school. It was tempting to have the Army pay for specialty schooling. The Army specialty program required four years pay back after the two years in school. That meant I would not be eligible to get out of army until I had twelve or more years active duty. If I had gone that route, I think I would have remained in the Army until I had served twenty years, retired as a bird colonel, and then started a private practice. Life would have been vastly different raising the children while in the military.

Pearl and I didn't especially want to raise our children, moving every three or four years to different military bases. Many "Army Brats" as they call kids who grow up in military surroundings turn out very well, as with Jay and Gloria Nichols' four boys. Pearl really liked the security of the military. We made the choice to separate from the Army and raise the children in one area. The only door open for me to become an orthodontist was the preceptorship program. I wrote several letters to orthodontists before I left the Army, asking if they were interested in me as a preceptor. Dr. Walter Appel in Cheyenne, Wyoming agreed to accept me for the three-year program.

The American Association of Orthodontists and the Rocky Mountain Society of Orthodontists approved our preceptor program so we moved to Cheyenne in July 1962. We started to buy a lovely home and settled into a nice new life. In October, I received several phone calls from Dr. Gillespie in Fairfield, California telling me that the Pacific Coast Society of Orthodontists and the AAO would soon be starting a new preceptorship class. Dr. Gillespie said that he and I had been approved to be part of that class. I knew I would get better training with Dr. Gillespie and his partner Dr. Bill Coon, so I paid back salary money that Dr. Appel had paid to me.

It was difficult to leave after three months, however I felt I wanted to be the best orthodontist I could be and that better training would pay off. Our family traveled 1,260 miles to Fairfield in our VW bug. Pearl held Craig all the way on her lap. Our dog, Diamond traveled with us. It was humorous the way we looked, being so crowded in the small car. People laughed at us from another car as we stopped at our first traffic light. Pearl finally gave an ultimatum that either the dog got shipped or she wouldn't go.

We tried to rent a cage to ship the dog, but there was a National Dog Show and no cages were available. The kids took a quick vote and told Pearl the dog had to come with us, and she reluctantly agreed to continue. Pearl was always a good sport. Diamond really was a wonderful dog, who lived for sixteen years. We didn't even pay any money for her. Everyone in our family loved the dog and the dog was very obedient. I took Mark and Diamond pheasant hunting and found out that I wasn't a good dog trainer. Diamond was more interested in chasing any bird or mouse that came along, instead of helping me put a pheasant on the table to eat. Diamond was a good watchdog, and the kids, especially Scott, played with her often.

The Army paid for our move to Cheyenne but we had to pay for the move to Fairfield. We got rid of a lot of stuff to make the move

144

less expensive. We backed out of the purchase of the house as the loan hadn't been completed and gave the owner an extra month's rent for the inconvenience of losing a buyer. Then off we went on another new adventure to Fairfield, California in October, 1962. It was the same time as the Cuban Missile Crises, a time when we almost had a nuclear war with the Soviet Union.

Gus G. Angelos

Fairfield

W hen we arrived in Fairfield, Dr. Gillespie was supposed to have found a house for us to rent. He hadn't followed through, and we ended up buying a house without any time to look around. I wasn't very pleased about that. We used up all of our savings on the move and house purchase. It was another time for economic belt tightening.

I started to work for Dr. Gillespie and Dr. Bill Coon, who was Joel's partner. They had two offices: one in Fairfield and one in Vallejo, which was twenty-five miles away. I worked two days in Vallejo and three days in Fairfield. Between the two doctors and their big practices, it proved to be an excellent opportunity to learn. They had a bigger and much more up to date practice with more and better equipment that Dr. Appel had in Cheyenne.

It turned out that the class of nine preceptors didn't officially start for another eighteen months after I arrived. Dr. Coon, Dr. Gillespie, and I had a verbal agreement that after three years in the practice I would be considered a fully trained orthodontist. I would then become an official partner and buy into the practice over the next three years. We didn't put it in writing and this came back to haunt me. After the three years when I was officially "trained," I still couldn't get an Orthodontic Certificate for another year and a half. When I started, Dr. Coon and Dr. Gillespie were each taking home over $52,000.00 a year, which was a large amount of money in those days. I was dreaming of making some big bucks.

My starting salary was $450.00 a month with a $50.00 raise every 3 months. We always lived on a budget and were financially behind all our dental friends. The Preceptor Program was excellent for clinical experience but weak in basic sciences and literature review. The program was better for me financially because I had an income and I didn't have to pay any tuition money. A big part of the learning depended on what kind of a practice you were in, and how good the doctor was. In my case I had two doctors. Dr. Gillespie was excellent with treatment while Dr. Coon was excellent with administrative business. The preceptorship program was instituted due to a shortage of school programs and the shortage of trained orthodontists in the country. I believe the program was in effect for about ten years and then discontinued as the school programs expanded.

I think some orthodontists from school programs tended to look down on those who trained as preceptees as second-class orthodontists. That is one reason I took the American Board Certification Exam as soon as I could. I was in two orthodontic study groups while in Fairfield. Gillespie's group had eight older established and respected orthodontists. The other group had six recent graduates from different schools, and the men were about my age. I couldn't have had a better study group situation. Joel was one of the smartest men I have ever known and was a gifted teacher. The downside was trying to spend enough time with him to study and review information. He would make about three or four appointments for teaching purposes and cancel a good number of them before we finally would get together. Everybody loved Joel because of his quick wit and magnetic personality. One of the ward ladies said he could charm the birds out of the trees, and that was the way Joel was.

Dr. George Hahn was a legend in his time in the field of orthodontics and was the chairman of the Preceptorship Program of the Pacific Coast Society of Orthodontists (PCSO). He was also the national chairman of the program for the AAO. Dr. Hahn had achieved everything possible in the field of orthodontics starting in the 1920's. He was one of the few living pioneers of modern orthodontics. He really liked Dr. Gillespie and me.

To meet the requirements of the program, we had to take a written and oral exam once a year at the University of California, write two papers after reviewing the literature on specific subjects, write a thesis, and show complete records of fifteen orthodontic cases that I treated. Candidates had to have some thing like 1,800 hours of extra training. I graduated number one in the class of nine. Many years later, Dr. Hahn saw me at a national orthodontic convention and introduced me to a group of his elite doctor friends. He put his arm around me and said I was the number one boy to come out of the PCSO program, which had about 130 men complete the program before it was discontinued. That was one of the nicest compliments I've ever had. Coming from Dr. Hahn it really meant a lot to me.

Fairfield was a great place to live. There were many outstanding Air Force Families. The Viet Nam War was going full blast and Travis Air Force Base was the main staging area to ship men and supplies over seas. We had about ten families that had children at about the same age as ours, and there was a

Virgil on right with our kids at Lake Powell

great abundance of talented, good LDS people around as well. Midway through our stay in Fairfield, the ward was divided. I was the elder's quorum president and when the 2nd Ward was organized, I was made the second counselor in the bishopric. Pearl was always busy working in the Primary with outstanding ladies and she loved it.

Everybody really loved Pearl. People have since told us that it was a Camelot time in Fairfield. Many of our good friends were in the other ward, which made us sad. On a few occasions, we went to San Francisco to see a musical or something special like the San Francisco Giants play baseball. The "City" is a great place to visit. Mark managed to go to a different school each year we were in Fairfield due to boundary changes and our one move to a nicer house. Sue started elementary school there and took care of Scott when he started school. Sue was always so good to look after her brothers. Sue was asked to help with the school lunch program because she was such an outstanding young girl. It was funny to see her standing on a stool working with the ladies in the kitchen. Sue was an outstanding athlete from day one. It is too bad that there wasn't very much for girls in organized sports programs as Sue was growing up.

Even in college, the programs were small. In Fairfield, Sue played softball in a league for girls from ten to sixteen years of age. I told Sue to ask for a tryout even though she was only nine years old at the time. She made the team and was the star player. Sue showed her athletic ability by making the all-star team. It was funny to see all the players who were fifteen and sixteen years of age and so much bigger, and then there was little nine-year-old Sue. We had good ward softball and basketball teams.

I also played in the county recreation fast pitch softball league. One year I just missed having the highest batting average in the county recreation league. I needed one more hit. The last year in Fairfield, I played on a team that won the city championship. I was thirty-six years old at the time and ten years older than anyone else on the team.

Mark played his first little league baseball games in Fairfield. We went to Golden Gate Park once, and Craig had a good size crowd watching him as he hit the whiffle ball. We would do that for exercise and entertainment. No one had ever seen a two or three year old kid who could hit like Craig. Scott got the nickname of "Huckle Hound" because of his association with and interest in our dog, his fun curiosity, and observations of nature. It was a nice time for our family.

Our vacations were mainly driving to Salt Lake to visit the family. It was best to drive all night so the kids could sleep. I would take the back seat out of the VW Beetle and put suitcases and a pad to make a bed in the back of the car.

One time Mark woke up in the middle of the night and said, "Dad do you think we can get a bigger car someday? It's pretty crowded back here and hard to sleep."

That was typical of Mark's sweet spirit and personality. Isn't that a nice way to ask for a bigger car – not a big complaint from a nine-year-old boy who shared the back of a Beetle with three siblings?

The following year we were able to buy a used Ford station wagon. I don't know how many times I drove all night between Salt Lake City and California. It was hard because it would always be after a full day of school or work, followed by a big rush to get on our way. Fortunately we never had an accident or any car trouble during our nine-year stay in California. After three years in practice, when it was time to become a partner according to our oral agreement, I was told that Joel and Bill Coon were splitting up the practice and would not be partners any longer. Joel would take the Fairfield office, and Bill would take the Vallejo office. I would continue to work in both offices. The break up was done in a very friendly way, and it was probably for the best except for me. They both benefited from the partnership of eight years because of different strengths. Joe told me he would make it up to me, as I was very disappointed. I didn't have my certificate and didn't have much of a bargaining position. I was able to negotiate a raise, but it was much less that what I would have made under our original agreement.

In 1967, as I neared the end of my official training and readied to get my certificate, Joel offered a deal for me to become partners and open a second office in Vacaville. It was a very tempting offer and time proved it would have been very lucrative. That area of California was growing fast. Pearl and I decided that we didn't want to stay in Fairfield to practice or raise our children. Joel felt bad about that. He understood we wanted to live in Salt Lake City.

George Gray had settled in Hemet, California and was building a second new office building. We visited him and his family in Hemet, which looked like a very nice place to settle down. George took me to meet all the dentists in Hemet. Twelve out of the fifteen dentists in the area were LDS, and I got to know them all. The only orthodontist there was a man I knew as an instructor in dental school, who was moving to San Bernardino. All the dentists, including the orthodontist, wanted me to come to Hemet. It would have been a place with a big readymade practice. I could have made a great deal of money in Hemet. History proved that to be the case. Other orthodontists had looked the area over, but all the dentists told the inquiring orthodontists that I was coming to Hemet and they were going to support me by sending me their orthodontic patients. George was one of the first dentists in the area and the leader of the group. He had influenced them all to support me. No other orthodontist was brought onto the practice until I decided not to practice there. It only took three months for someone to take my place. Now there are five orthodontists practicing in Hemet and George tells me they are all busy.

By the fall of 1966, George had 75 consultations lined up for me. All the other dentists had patients waiting who needed orthodontic treatment. The area was ripe and ready to harvest. During the summer of 1966, we took a trip to Salt Lake City to visit our family. We always stayed at the Trauffer's home. Their house was bigger than my parents. Pearl also liked it better there. One evening after the kids were in bed, Pearl and I went to Snelgroves ice cream store for a milk shake. Dr. Bill Bosworth and his wife were there. We knew them and sat together and had a nice visit. Bill told me that I should come to Salt Lake, as they really needed another orthodontist in Sugarhouse. He would refer patients to me and was sure he could get some of his close friends to do likewise.

On the way back to Fairfield, I told Pearl that I thought Salt Lake was the best place for us to live and raise our family. She was happy beyond words. I knew I wouldn't make as much money in Utah and that it would take much longer to build a practice. That remains true to this day. We discussed it and prayed about it, and made the decision to go to Salt Lake. I never did tell Joel about Hemet.

When I told him we wanted to go to Salt Lake, he was disappointed but understood. Joel kept offering better financial deals, hoping for me to stay, up to the time we left. He offered for me to come to work one week a month while I started up a practice in Salt Lake. I was grateful for the offer and traveled to Fairfield for six months. Joel was nice enough to have me stay at his house. This turned out to be beneficial for Joel and a financial lifesaver for me. Starting a practice from scratch means no positive cash flow for a period of time. Joel needed time to get an associate with the big Fairfield practice.

In May 1967 we traveled by car to Salt Lake City. We moved into the Trauffer home at 970 Ramona Ave. in Sugarhouse. I opened an office at 1261 Wilmington Avenue, in Sugarhouse. It was a small office, but things went well. I felt bad because the move caused Sue to miss the only day of school that she had ever missed, including nursery school. That speaks well for Sue and her health. What a girl.

Our three younger children went to Forest school, which was the same elementary school that Pearl had gone to. Mark went to Irving, which had been Pearl's junior high school as well. During our first year in Salt Lake, Jay Nichols was sent to Thailand with the Air Force for a one-year

152

tour of duty. Gloria and their four boys lived one block away during that year. The cousins really got to know each other and had a great year going to school, church, and playing with each other. We bought our first home in Salt Lake the following summer. It was a nice brick home located at 990 Millcreek Way. That was a wonderful area with lots of kids the same age as our kids. It was especially good for Sue, as she had a group of about eight girls who were good gals, although they couldn't get along very well at times. Sue was the force that united them into a close group of wonderful teenage girls.

Lake Powell camping in isolated area, Scott has our dog- Diamond

The Grant 12th Ward was very good for all of us. Pearl and I had many callings in the ward and I eventually became the first Counselor to Bishop Deal Griggs. We lived there for six years and had wonderful friends. We had a good family life doing typical family things. We bought a second-hand boat with another family, started water skiing, and travelling to Lake Powell. The whole family loved the water skiing outings around Salt Lake as well as Lake Powell. The kids got to be good water skiers. The children participated in many little league sports and did well in everything. I coached all the boys in little league baseball and/or football. I always participated on the ward basketball and softball teams.

We got into snow skiing as a family. Pearl was always great to support the whole family in everything. She even tried to water ski a couple of times. She didn't like the cold and it bothered her asthma, so she never bothered with snow skiing. I got the kids into tennis and we had some fun times. The kids never did really stay with tennis, as they got older. Pearl always worked long and hard to get things ready, take care of food, and clean up for any family activities. Scott and his tender heart led us into accepting a Navaho Indian boy named Virgil Manning to live with us for two years. His age was between Craig and Scotts. There was an Indian Placement Program sponsored by the LDS Church. The purpose of the program was to try to give the young Indian children a better education, provide more opportunities, and help them to do better in society away from the reservation. It was interesting to have another young man live with us and to treat him like one of our own children.

Virgil was a nice, pleasant boy. It was difficult to motivate him in school, however. He loved to ski and we hit on the idea to have him take a paper to each class on Friday and have the teacher sign that he had done his homework and classwork. If he did these things, we took him skiing each Saturday. His grades were quite good during ski season and he never missed going skiing. Everyone, especially his teacher, was happy about that. The Indian Placement Program was discontinued after about ten years. Pearl and I always hoped that we had done some good for Virgil and that we may have planted some seeds that would help him in the future. Virgil came by my office about ten years after he graduated from high school. He was married and had two little girls. He was a mechanic and was unemployed. He also said he had a drinking (alcohol) problem. I gave him some money.

In June 2005, Pearl got on the internet, looked for Virgil, and found his address. I wrote a letter to Virgil and he phoned a few weeks later. We had a wonderful conversation with him. He had divorced his wife. They remarried a few years later and had another daughter who was sixteen years old at the time. The older two girls were in college. Virgil worked as a director in a funeral home in New Mexico and said he enjoyed it. He was in the Elders Quorum presidency and said everything was really going along well. Virgil said he would be traveling from New Mexico to Salt Lake and would look us up during the summer of 2005. It seemed as though the seeds we had hoped to plant with Virgil grew into something nice.

In 2007, Virgil and his family came to our house for a visit. It was a wonderful reunion. His family was very active in Church and doing well. They all looked good.

My practice grew and went along very well. I took the American Board of Orthodontics Exams and became board certified in 1975. At that time, about one-third of all the orthodontists in the country were board certified. It was a very big process. First, there was a six-hour written exam and then I had to display complete records on fifteen patients that I had treated. This meant that for each patient, I needed to have three sets of oral x-rays, three x-rays of the head, three sets of photos, and three sets of plaster study models of the teeth. These records had to be over at least a six-year period. I also had to have complete write-ups on all fifteen cases. And finally, I was given an oral exam by seven examiners. The grading was all done without anyone knowing your identity, except for the oral exam. There were ninety candidates that passed the exam that year with about fifteen people that failed. Of those who passed the exam, ten of the most outstanding were asked to show their cases at the following National Orthodontic Meeting held in New York City. I was very fortunate to be one of the ten asked to show their cases. Not many orthodontists are ever honored to have that experience. Simply put, it meant I was one of the best of the best. Taking and passing the board was something I wanted to do to prove that I was as good at orthodontics as the next orthodontist.

Being a Board Certified Orthodontist was an important goal to me. Before I came to Salt Lake, Dr. George Hahn, who I wrote about earlier, had told some of the top established orthodontists in Utah about a "good boy coming to practice in Salt Lake, whose name was Gus." By giving me his endorsement, I think I was accepted much better as a new-comer in the orthodontic community.

When I flew to St. Louis for the main part of the board exam, I had two large cardboard boxes that contained all my records. The whole family took me to the airport and we looked around the airport at displays. When I finally went to board the plane, I was informed the flight was overbooked and that they would get me on another flight soon. As I had checked-in the boxes earlier, I was very concerned that the valuable material would be safely cared for when the plane got to St. Louis ahead of me. There was absolutely no way those x-rays and plaster models and items could ever be replaced. They were only valuable to me and represented work and materials done over a ten-year period of time. The airline people made phone calls and assured me that the boxes would be picked up and cared for. When I arrived at St. Louis, I was late and the boxes were set in an isle where people were walking around them. No one had cared for them. Anyone could have taken them as they were away from the counter.

I grabbed them, grabbed a cab, and rushed to my hotel a little late and very stressed, but okay. That day I learned a lesson about flying on airlines and how to avoid stress – be sure to check in and confirm your seat assignment first, so you don't get bumped off the plane.

In 1978, I discovered that my trusted office girl, Rose Mary Lamb, who had worked for me since I started in Salt Lake, had been embezzling money from me for 11½ years. She had worked for Dr. Coon and Dr. Gillespie for two years and had been a very good employee. I made a big mistake and trusted her completely. It is a long sad story. She embezzled $150,000.00. She admitted her guilt and spent six months in prison. She never returned any of the money.

The civil court case took five years and was very complicated because Rosie had passed most of the money on to her husband and then they had gotten divorced. They had bought six rental properties and renovated them with the stolen money. The bank had allowed her to deposit my business checks into her private account, which was against the banking laws. She forged my name and then added hers on all the checks. She also took all the cash, which could never be traced. When the case was over, I got $75,000.00 from the bank and $1,500.00 from the former husband. No money from Rosie. My legal expenses were $71,000.00.

The tax rules at the time were such that the following year I had to pay an extra $20,000.00 in income tax. I would have been better off not going to court or believing what my attorney had told me about how much money could be recovered. My attorney was a very nice, soft-spoken man who didn't have much experience in trial cases. He did wills and trusts and things like that. It would have been much better for me if I had hired a tough, hard-nosed experienced trial attorney. Too often the attorneys are paid for their services and there isn't any money left for the victims. This case generated over $250,000.00 in legal fees. One can get a ruling in court but it may not be justice. In the end, I was happy that I could keep the money that I had earned from that point forward. I felt bad for the whole situation. Had the embezzlement not taken place, I would have put most of that money away for retirement.

I wouldn't have changed our living standard except to take better vacations and probably not had to wait until 1975 to purchase a new car. When Scott was set apart for his mission to New Zealand, President Partridge said, "Your family will be blessed commensurate with your diligence in the mission field." I believe it was one of the blessings of Scott being on a mission that I found out about the embezzlement. Nevertheless, it was another lesson learned in the school of hard knocks. There was one positive thing that came out of the whole thing – getting a large sum of money at that exact time allowed us to help Sue and Mark Young acquire their first McDonalds Restaurant in Park City. We had loaned them a large sum of money, which they paid back with interest.

After six years in our home on Millcreek Way, we thought about remodeling and adding to our home. One thing led to another, and we finally wound up moving to another house rather than remodel. We moved in May, 1973, into our present home at 3653 Hermes Drive in the Mt. Olympus area. That was our twentieth move since we were married. We have been here for over thirty years. It was a very good move and had a profound effect on our children and those who they eventually married.

Mark, Sue, and Craig married people they had met in this area. Scott really connected with a great group of young men and met Shelly through his friends here, even though she lived in St. George. All four of our children did a wonderful job picking their spouses. Our family rule was that the boys should be at least twenty-four years of age and Sue should be twenty-two years old before they got married. They all did this. During this period in time, couples were getting married younger than the ages that our children got married. Marriage is one of the most important decisions one makes in life. Many times Pearl and I have told our grandchildren this fact. I hope they listened.

As our kids grew up, they gave us much joy and happiness. Fortunately, no one had any big problems of any kind. All our children developed a good work ethic. This is one of the challenges that parents face, to teach kids to be good workers. If they have been taught a good work ethic, along with a good value system, kids will generally be okay in life. We tried very hard to always know where our children were and whom they were with. We had lots of rules and the kids obeyed them. Craig tested the rules the most, but learned to live with our rules. I believe it helped our children to learn to obey rules by starting in early childhood and being consistent.

We held Family Home Evening every Monday, which really helped bond our family together. Moving also helped to bond us together. We did lots of fun things together as a family. Everyone was healthy and did well in school. All the kids loved sports, and did well in them, even to the point that Sue and Craig had athletic scholarships in college. The kids and I always did lots of snow skiing. Riding the old, slow two-chair ski lifts, turned out to be a real bonus for me. We would take turns riding with each person for the six to fifteen minutes ride to the top of the mountain. This was one-on-one time for me to spend with each of the children. It was precious beyond words. The new, rapid ski lifts that carry four to six people have changed that special opportunity. I remember only one time that I had one-on-one time with my father and that was only about one half hour total.

Scott, Mark Y, and Gus

An Autobiography

Pearl was always there when the kids came home from school, would talk to them, and help them with anything. She also waited up for them to come home at night, as they got older. There was always a certain time to be home and the kids were good about that.

We took lots of vacations together. Our family really enjoyed going to Lake Powell each year to water ski and enjoy the beautiful scenery. We have done this since 1972. Pearl also has worked hard to have family reunions. Our kids know all of their cousins pretty well, even though they live in various places throughout the country.

When the kids were young, I took them deer hunting, but I never shot a deer when they were along. It was a camping trip more than a hunting trip. None of the kids wanted to continue to hunt, as they got older. For about six years, I did have some wonderful hunting experiences in Wyoming with a friend named Frank Oldroyd. He had horses and a little camping trailer. It was plush to hunt with horses and sleep in a heated trailer, rather than a tent. Frank grew up and knew the Wyoming area, and we always got an elk or moose. It was like going with a professional outfitter – all that I had to do was furnish the food and gas. Frank was a good man to be around. Elk and Moose meat is much better than deer meat. Eventually I gave up hunting because I felt sorry for the animals. If I ever shot anything, I always ate it.

Mark injured his knee playing football when he was a sophomore at Granite High School. I have always felt bad because I took him to a doctor who was a friend and a family practitioner, not a specialist. The knee seemed to be healing up, and then he injured it again. Eventually, the knee was operated on, and the cartilage was removed. I should have taken him to a specialist first. Now days, the treatment would be much better. I coached and helped all the kids in many sports.

We still go to Lake Powell once a year and invite any of our family members who are available to join us. Now we rent trailers, which are like mobile homes, and have an easier time with air conditioning, stoves, fridges, and beds. I really liked it when we slept on the sandy beaches and roughed it far away from everyone. However, as the grandchildren that needed bottles, diapers, and naps came along, things changed. I like the 'easy way' now.

159

Gus G. Angelos

We rented a houseboat once and took Pearl's parents and my mom to Lake Powell. Lake Powell vacations are some of my favorite family memories. To get away from everyone and everything in such a beautiful scenic area with family is my idea of a great vacation. Everybody gets along well and the grandchildren are happy to see each other on these trips. The stars are more visible at Lake Powell than anywhere. Boating vacations are still appealing to everyone in our family regardless of age. I got spoiled with the warm smooth water to ski in at Lake Powell. I quit water skiing in the Salt Lake City reservoirs years ago because the water was cold, and rough due to too many boats. The equipment has changed over the years and now one can keep warm with wet and/or dry suits.

Our family went to lots of games in which the kids participated. One time, when Craig was playing little league football and Scott was waiting to play the next game, a scary thing happened. There was snow on the ground and it was cold. One of the other coaches brought a salamander heater to keep the players warm. During our half time, the head coach and I were talking to Craig's team in the end zone. Suddenly, I heard an explosion and turned to see a man with his hair burning. Worse still, Scott was totally engulfed in flames and was twirling around and fell to the ground. It looked like something you'd see on a TV show. It was a horrible thing to see.

I ran as fast as I could to Scott and put out the last of the flames. After being knocked to the ground, Scott had rolled on the wet ground and put out most of the flames. I don't think I ever ran faster in my life. I was about fifty yards away and the first one to reach Scott. The problem arose when one of the coaches asked Scott to hold a lid up while he put some fuel oil in the heater's tank. The five-gallon can contained gas instead of regular fuel, which exploded. Fortunately Scott had on extra clothing besides his football uniform with pads, so he only had a small burn on the shin of his leg. An ambulance was called. Scott wanted me to go with him to the hospital. He was examined and then released. Scott was about thirteen years old and handled that experience very well. We were all extremely happy nothing worse came out of that experience.

The only other time I took anyone to the emergency room was when Sue fell playing volleyball. She was about thirteen years old. She needed a few stitches for a cut on her leg.

160

An Autobiography

In high school, Mark put his time and energy into the Madrigals singing group. His knee injury precluded any further participation in sports. Years later, we found that Mark had some real talent in swimming and distance running. Ralph Rogers got him into vocal music and it turned out to be a very good experience. Mark had a nice part in Granite High School's musical his senior year. The musical was The Sound of Music and Mark was the telegram delivery boy. He was also the senior class vice president.

Mark was an excellent student. In the second grade the principal of the school told me that Mark could become anything he wanted because he was so bright. Mark decided at age thirteen that he wanted to be a medical doctor and he never looked back. He had the most organized plan anyone could imagine. Mark did all of his college schooling at the University of Utah. He rode the bus to school, worked as a teaching assistant, and worked at other places to help with his school expenses. He really zeroed-in on what he wanted then worked hard to achieve his M. D. degree.

Sue helped me at the office during the summers from the time she was twelve years old. She was always a delight to have around and a very good worker. I was extremely pleased she chose to become a dental hygienist. She excelled in basketball and volleyball at Granite High School. Girls' team sports weren't very big at that time, so basketball and volleyball were the only girls' team sports that played against other high schools. There weren't many spectators at the girls' games. After one year at the University of Utah, Sue went to Sheridan Junior College in Sheridan, Wyoming and obtained a degree in Dental Hygiene. At that time, no school in Utah offered dental hygiene, so Sue was forced to go out of state. She was the star on the basketball and volleyball teams at Sheridan College. She also played on the tennis team for the school, even though she hadn't played a great deal of tennis. Sue's experience in Sheridan was similar to a Church mission. She was the only LDS girl on any of the teams and had different standards than the rest of the girls.

One time, when the basketball team won a tournament in Nebraska, all of the girls on the team went into a bar to celebrate. Sue stayed at the motel, and the girls brought her a bouquet of flowers, which showed a lot of class and how much the girls like her.

Scott worked at my office doing lab work. He was very talented with anything related to mechanics, art or music. He painted an outstanding oil painting in the ninth grade. That painting is still my favorite painting. It hangs in our front room. Scott and his group really had fun playing ward basketball and softball. They had very good teams. Scott had a tough break with school basketball. His age group had some outstanding players who had played together for quite a few years. They were talented and won the state basketball championship two years. He was the last guy cut when trying out for the school team. Scott wrestled on Skyline's school wrestling team and did very well, especially being new to the sport.

When all of Scott's friends came home from their missions, I played on the Ward slow pitch softball team with them. We had a great team. I was the only old player and all the kids were good athletes. We always won the stake softball league and went a long way in many tournaments. One year we won everything, but then the guys started to get married one-by-one and moved away. Scott, Mark Young, once in a while Craig, and I played in the County Recreation slow pitch league for quite a few years. Again, I was twenty-five years older than the next oldest player who was Mark Young. When our County Recreation team disbanded, I was sixty years old.

Another team phoned me and asked me to play with them. That was a real ego trip because I was just a shell of a player at that time, but still a team thought I could help them out. I decided not to play any longer in the county recreation league because Scott and Mark were not going to continue playing.

There are a couple of positions that older guys can play with young guys. I could pitch quite well and could hit the ball in the area left open by the fielders. I always had a higher batting average than half the young guys on the team.

One year for some unknown reason the officials picked the most valuable player on each team for a special game. I happened to be lucky that game and was picked as the player on our team and given a gift certificate. Most players on our team were better than me, but it was a nice 'last hurrah' type of experience. I had fun kidding the rest of the team about that. I really enjoyed playing with Scott, Mark, and Craig when he could make it.

I played ten more years with our ward team but finally quite when we couldn't get enough players for a ward team. By then, the ward teams were not very good, especially compared to the county recreation league. I always enjoyed the friendships and association playing on ball teams.

In 2002, our bishop asked me to get a team together and coach them. I was very happy to gather enough players that I didn't have to play also. By the time you reach age seventy, you aren't much of a softball player, especially to compete against young men. That was true for me. I had had my day and was very lucky to go as long as I did. There is a time and a season for all things and it was time for me to move on to another sport like golf, and of course, continue to ski as often as possible.

From day one, Craig was a very good athlete. I never worried about his performance. He had a great gift for any sport and knew what to do as well as when and how. He excelled from little

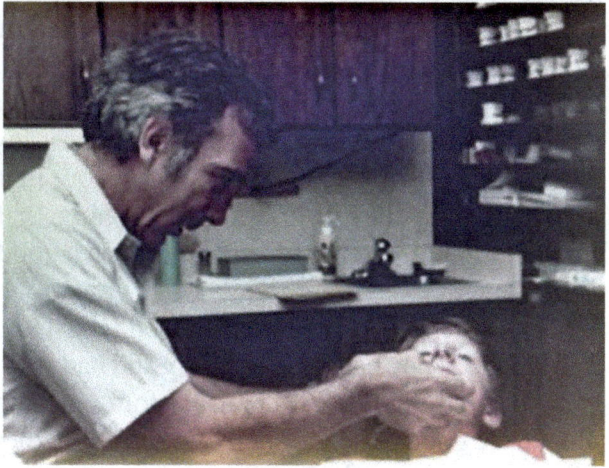

Typical day enjoying work

league sports through college. When we moved to the house we are living in as I write this memoir, we took Craig to sign up for little league football. Craig was in the sixth grade at the time. The coach asked him what position he played at the sign up. The coach rolled his eyes when Craig told him he was another quarterback. However, it took only a short time before Craig was the star quarterback.

There was a large group of talented athletes in Craig's age group. Those kids played together during the Little League years and hardly ever lost a game. They won the State Football Championship in high school as the first undefeated team that Skyline ever had. By then Craig was the running back. He was the Tribune newspaper's Most Valuable Player for the 1980 All State Football Team, which was made up of players from the largest high schools. Craig was also the starting point guard and shortstop on Skyline's teams. He was All-State in football and baseball. It was fun to watch him. It was a real blessing that all the best players of the football championship team were good Mormons. There wasn't any drinking, bad language, or inappropriate behavior to contend with. Too often that isn't the case on athletic teams.

These players all worked hard and had a great experience. Craig always stood up for the underdog. Craig had charisma and the kids looked up to him. The seminary teacher told me that once in a while, Craig would tell the class to shape up and they would do it better for him than for the instructor. Craig was picked the most outstanding boy athlete at Skyline high school his senior year.

All of our children have been very special to raise – it has been a real privilege to be their parent. The greatest joy and accomplishment of my life has been to be the father to these four incredible human beings and to see how well they have turned out. I hope that Pearl and I have formed a good foundation for them and have been a good example to influence the future generations of our family.

Our children were always well adjusted to our moves or whatever came along. They have been healthy and had very few accidents or injuries. I was thrilled that I could treat our four children's orthodontic problems. They were good patients and it was fun to see them on a professional basis. All four have beautiful smiles and healthy mouths. They all associated with good friends and had lots of varied interests. Pearl and I were always as involved as we could be with their activities.

Pearl was active in PTA and was the PTA president at most of the schools the kids attended. She was a volunteer teacher's aid and helped out with numerous projects at all of the kids' schools. No one has been a better church worker than Pearl. She was a volunteer for twenty years at the University Hospital and had provided some incredible service for neighbors and friends. Much of this service has been done without any fanfare and with very few people knowing about most of it. But, the family came first.

As each of our children reached the stage of life to get married, I thought it might be nice as parents to pick out the spouses for our children, like was done in olden times. As it worked out, each of our children did

164

much better than I could have done picking their spouse. All of our children got married in the Salt Lake Temple and their grandfather Walter Trauffer performed the marriages. That was another special family experience. I could not have written a script for better children. All of our children have been a joy to be around. They all made good decisions through out their lives. Each one of them has a college degree. They all have been very strong in the Church from day one. All three boys are Eagle Scouts, and have received Duty to God Awards. Sue got all the awards given to Young Women. Each one of the boys went on a mission: Mark to Switzerland, Scott to New Zealand, and Craig to Virginia. Sue's husband, Mark Young served a mission to Toronto, Canada. Each one of their spouses has a college degree.

All of our grandchildren have had stay-at-home moms during all their formative years. To date, all of my grandsons, with the exception of two have become Eagle Scouts. The two who are not Eagle Scouts got close, but were too isolated from an organized troop. Our oldest grandson, Tyler completed a mission to Honduras. Matt Young went to South Dakota, Ryan Angelos went to the Dominion Republic, Bryant Angelos went to Peru, Jordan went to Finland, Spencer Young went to Washington State, Kyle Angelos went to Arizona, Nick Angelos to Ghana, and Carter to Florida. I believe that most of my twelve grandsons will complete honorable missions for the Church. They are very good kids and time will tell what they do with their lives.

Our genealogy sheets show how many children each family has and the related details. Our children have become excellent parents and all nineteen grandchildren are healthy and happy. They are bright children, are doing well in school, have many interests, involved in varied activities, and are well adjusted. They are also strong in the gospel. I think all the grandchildren are good-looking too. That may be the opinion of a typical grandfather, but if anyone is interested, he can look at pictures of the family and judge for himself. Facial anatomy, balanced structure, and features are very important for an orthodontist to know about, so I write with some knowledge and much expertise on the matter of facial features and looks.

To date, most the older grandchildren have had orthodontic treatment, which makes me happy. I was very happy to treat Sue's two older children, Matt and Amy, and Scott's oldest, Mandy. I wished I could have taken care of all the grandchildren's orthodontic needs, but distance and retirement made that impossible.

All of our children have done well in their chosen careers. Mark Angelos is a full professor and medical doctor at Ohio State University. Sue and Mark Young own six McDonalds Restaurants located in Park City, Utah, Heber, Utah, and Evanston, Wyoming. In 2007 they acquired two more restaurants in Cedar City, Utah. Sue was a successful Dental Hygienist but quit when she became a mother. Scott owns three McDonalds Restaurants located in Goodland, Kansas, Burlington, Colorado, and Lamar, Colorado. Scott changed careers from being a chemical engineer. Scott and his family spent three years in India at a new glass factory. He was successful as a chemical engineer. Scott changed his career and decided to go the McDonalds route after India. Craig is an attorney and is the Athletic Director at Florida Atlantic University. He worked a few years at the N.C.A.A. headquarters and was then offered a job at the University of Miami when they had problems with the N.C.A.A. Craig was the number-two man in the Athletic Department at Miami University for eight years, and Indiana University for one year.

I have never personally known a family where the parents have been so lucky to have their children and grandchildren turn out so good. Needless to say, Pearl and I are extremely proud of them. We don't say anything to friends because most families have had problems and unhappiness somewhere along the line with their children or grandchildren. We don't wish to boast or sound proud to anyone. So far, we have been blessed beyond words. We hope and pray that it continues.

I retired from orthodontics and sold my practice when I was seventy years old. The last patient that I saw was in the summer of 2000. I practiced dentistry and orthodontics for forty-three years. It was a great profession for my family and me. It is a demanding profession. It gave me the opportunity to perform a health service as well as make pretty smiles. If the teeth fit together properly, chances are you will keep them all your life with minimum upkeep and expense. Orthodontics and dentistry can help change people's lives by giving them a better appearance and improved self-esteem. I always felt strongly that orthodontics was an excellent investment in a healthier mouth as well as a better smile.

During the formative years, one's appearance is important. At times

I could see a big improvement in self-esteem with some of my patients. Sometimes parents would tell me that orthodontic treatment changed the live of their child. Most orthodontic patients are young adolescents, still trying to discover who they are. They have all of life's big decisions ahead of them. Most of the kids I worked on came from good families and were good kids. It gave me a chance to have a nice friendship with them. Generally I would see patients over a seven-year period of time.

Orthodontics provided my family and me with a good income. I never regretted becoming an orthodontist. Not only was it possible to be my own boss, I could choose to do charity work whenever I wanted to do so. Something that I never told our children was that each year at Christmas time, I would select fifteen or twenty patients and send their 109 parents a notice they did not have to make a monthly payment in December. I also dismissed any money owed to the office if a family had a big tragedy occur. I believe I got more satisfaction out of these kind deeds than any patient or their family did. Only Pearl and I shared these experiences.

As to retirement income, there was a concern that social security might not be around when I finally retired. I established a pension plan in the early years of my in practice and put money into the plan. I also decided that it would be wise to invest in rental properties for retirement purposes. That way, I figured I would have a good balanced retirement plan. I bought and sold around twenty-three different properties. This strategy worked out very well. It forced me to be a landlord for nearly thirty-three years, starting in 1972. I would like to have been able to purchase commercial properties or larger rental properties, and hire managers. Getting a late start and leaving California took away from our income, but I am a very firm believer that money isn't everything and it doesn't buy happiness. Having too much money at times creates big challenges and problems for parents and children.

Being a landlord of small residential properties had some drawbacks, but it worked out well for us. A triplex located at 1116 East 4th South and a duplex located at 1623 South 1400 East were properties that our oldest three children lived in while attending the University of Utah. This was a good way to help our children after they were married. I was also able to help some of my nieces and nephews who rented some of these properties by giving them reduced rent.

I traded out cement work, roofs, tile work, carpets, and things like that on the properties for orthodontic treatment. Bob Forsgren and I did lots of painting and repair work to keep the properties in good condition. Bob was very helpful and talented.

Another thing we did was to give all our children used cars, mostly Volkswagens. I was able to trade out the repairs on all of the Volkswagen cars each of our children owned. I drove Volkswagen cars for thirty years to hold down expenses. Not having to buy cars and repair them helped the kids when they were in college and newly married. My CPA told me occasionally that I did as well with my investments as any of his clients. He knew the financial information of many people, so I think that was a valid statement. As far as investments went, I did well on most, but also had some poor investments.

My intent was to help the kids out when they were young adults with their education, careers, and families. Now, our kids are all doing well and don't need any help. I firmly believe that everyone should experience some struggle to learn the value of hard work and sacrifice early in life. We all need to have a good value system and sort out the really important things in life. We learn our core values early in life, which is why family and home are so important. I believe it is wise to have worthwhile short-term and long-term goals and to make good decisions accordingly.

Knowing the difference between "wants" and "needs" is also important. The Book of Mormon illustrates over and over again the problems that can come with too much prosperity. I think our four children did very well in this area. I still pray daily for these values with our family. It is too bad that we don't learn at a young age to talk and consult with older people who have traveled along life's road to learn from their experiences and wisdom. I wish I would have done that more.

I think the American culture is centered too much on youth. Asian traditions and cultures emphasize respect and learning opportunities that can be gained from older people and family members. Times continue to change so perhaps it may someday come to pass in this country. In my early years when I was forming my core values, the great depression and World War II made my generation very independent and cooperative. I never liked to ask favors from anyone and to this day, I very seldom ask anyone to do me a favor. Each generation is different.

An Autobiography

My generation is named the silent generation. My parents' generation was very different from mine. Their generation had a harder life than my generation. Credit of any kind was hardly available during my early years. No credit cards. My generation had to save up to buy something. We just went without until we could afford things. I always paid my bills and took care of my obligations. I do not owe any money to anyone. As to finances, I recommend that people stay out of debt as much as possible and just go without if you can't afford something. You are always safe if you spend less than you make. And believe it or not, rainy days or hard times come to most people, so be prepared for the unexpected. I say hope for the best and expect the worst and have a good plan. Use common sense and examine your own wants and indulgences, as children learn from your example.

It seems to me that many people aren't clear as to what they really need as opposed to what they want or think they need. Please understand that these are the thoughts of an old conservative man.

Gus G. Angelos

Various Jobs and Thoughts as a Young Boy

I will list some of the jobs I had as a boy and as young man then give a brief explanation. Many of these jobs helped me mature and get a better understanding of what was required to be successful in life.

My wonderful father-in-law told me, "A man spends more time working and providing for his family than anything else."

I don't know anything about my pre-mortal life, so I don't know if I had a choice as to when or where I was born, or what was going on in the world. I am extremely glad that I was born after the gospel had been restored, and in the USA where I could easily hear it.

Socrates said, "The only thing constant in life is change." How true.

The Stock market crashed in October 1929, which was the month I was born. The Great Depression followed and lasted until the end of World War II. I was two months shy of age sixteen when Word War II ended. During the depression, times were hard. There were very few welfare programs. Social Security started in 1937, I think. Credit was very difficult to obtain. Unemployment rose to 25% of the work force during the Great Depression.

I lived in a middle class neighborhood, where less than half of the families had a car. No one had very much. Everyone did the best they could. Everyone except the oldest in each family wore hand-me-down clothes and went barefoot some of the time in the summer. Clothes were patched and worn out before being discarded. Toys were in short supply and shared by the whole family. Kids were happy and used their imaginations for games and entertainment.

Gus G. Angelos

I never had an allowance and rarely asked my mom for money. I was quite bashful as a kid and didn't like trying to hustle a job. However, I knew if I wanted money I had to earn it, and so I was always looking for a job to earn some money. I loved sports. As I got older, I could have worked more and not participated in sports. However, in the long run it worked out well to have an athletic scholarship for four years of college and make money, playing baseball – not to mention the enjoyment, and the many things I learned about life by participating in sports.   Sometimes boys had to work to help support the family. When that happened, they could not participate in athletics. Some boys even had to quit school to help their families financially. I was glad this didn't happen to me. As I mentioned earlier, twice my dad told me it might be better if I backed off from athletics some and get a job to earn money for college. Fortunately for me, my dad didn't insist on this.

No one at that time could imagine that baseball would enable me to obtain a college education and would have such a profound influence on my future. My father never said it, but one of his business friends told me how proud my dad was that I was able to play professionally and get a free college education from baseball. Things like that were unheard of in Greece.

I followed my dream to become a professional baseball player even though it was only for a short time. I also followed my dream to become an orthodontist. My earliest job to earn any money was as an errand boy, who would go to the grocery store for an invalid lady who lived across the street. I think I was about six or seven years of age. The lady would give me a small list of grocery items to buy, some money, and I would walk to the store to buy the items for her. She would then give me a nickel or a few pennies for payment. I always bought candy, as it was a real treat in those days. I could get seven caramels for a penny or two pieces of licorice for a penny.

I took handbills (advertisements) door to door for the local grocery store once in a while. I tried but never could get that as a steady job. There were no supermarkets, only small grocery stores. I delivered newspapers for a while as a helper to an older boy who owned the route. I tried to sell magazine subscriptions and was a poor door-to-door salesman. I think the magazines that I tried to sell were *Liberty and Ladies Home Companion*.

172

An Autobiography

As I recall, I only sold one subscription. I learned early on that I was not a good salesman.

I had some success knocking on doors in the neighborhood to ask people if I could mow their lawn. The price was twenty-five cents a yard. This meant using a hand lawn mower to cut the front and back yard grass, then raking it, and hand trimming the edges. A couple of times, I would use the twenty-five cents to ride the bus (five cents each way), ten cents for a movie, and a nickel for a candy bar. That was a big time treat. I did this alone because none of my friends had any money at the time. That was big stuff for an eleven year old.

My Brother and I worked at a bowling alley for a time, setting bowling pins by hand. This was before automatic pin setting machines existed.

During World War II Sam and I worked in Murray at a cannery that canned peas. We would ride the bus and start work at six p.m. then get off work at six in the morning. I think I only lasted a month or two on that summer job. I was thirteen or fourteen years old during that summer.

My first indoor job was to work at Johnson's Ice Cream for thirty-five cents an hour. I started as the dishwasher, quickly advanced to scooping ice cream, and then to making milk shakes, sundays, and stuff like that. That was a fun job because we could make any ice cream treat that we wanted, to eat after closing and cleaning was completed.

At age thirteen or fourteen, I worked a summer at Memory Grove cutting lawns. At age fifteen, I got a job at the brickyard, which was only three blocks from my home. I told them I was sixteen because that was the minimum age required to hire heavy labor workers. I had to join the union. The pay was 75 cents an hour. That was considered adult wages. Many of the older men supported their families on that wage. I worked there for about five different summers. It was hard work but it was big time money.

During the five years I worked at the brickyard, the war ended and there was a big change to mechanized equipment. We worked with shovels and wheel barrels to unload clay out of railroad cars. Once a week, I would help make bricks. I would personally handle 15,000 wet bricks that came off of a conveyor belt. For a month or two, I worked as a construction laborer building an elementary school that my future son-in-law, Mark Young eventually attended.

Sam and I worked as waiters for my dad when he had a small lunch stand on 9th South and Main Street in Salt Lake. I also was the dishwasher there.

I played on a softball team in a good league that Rudy and Headland Junkyard sponsored. I worked at the junkyard doing odd jobs part of one summer. It was fun to be around all of the cars.

While still in high school, one winter, I worked on weekends at Kennecott Copper Mine as a laborer on the mountain in deep snow. I think I only lasted a couple of months on that job. After I graduated from high school, I applied at the local union office to become a plumber's apprentice because two of my close friends were plumbers. There was a job offer if I could join the union. The union man asked me whether I had a dad or uncle who was a plumber and I said, "no." He told me there weren't any openings at that time and to come back in a year.

I had thought that being a plumber might be a good job to have during the "off season," particularly if I were to be a professional baseball player.

One Christmas, I worked at Z.C.M.I. (a church department store) packing china for shipping. After I started school at the University of Wyoming, I worked the first year at the Pi Bata Phi Sorority house in Laramie. This job included two meals a day and ten dollars per month. I didn't eat breakfast that year and managed to get by on two meals a day.

The next three years I did a small amount of work for my full-time scholarship, which was required by the NCAA. One year I was assigned to clean out the attic of the Athletic Dorm. I knew that job would be really easy because the other fellow assigned to that job was an All-American basketball player.

I went to the attic one time that year. I was in charge of a cleaning crew for five home football games the next year. We swept and cleaned up all the paper and stuff from a section in the football stadium. During my senior year, I took sandwiches and drinks to the people in the press box during the home football games. It was fun to see the radio people (no TV) and visiting coaches, who were scouting. It was also warm in the press box – some football games were played in cold bad weather. The NCAA required that student athletes work but most of the work was not real work.

An Autobiography

While paying summer baseball, I got paid for playing. I also worked full-time during two summers at a lumberyard, and one summer for the gas company in Worland, Wyoming. I worked two weeks in a meat packing company feeding cattle and doing odd jobs. I worked a few days at a gas station. I never went very long without some type of job.

In my fourth year at Wyoming, I came home on Christmas vacation and got a job selling Christmas trees. I enjoyed that even though it was an outside job in December. After I started dental school, I ushered the football games at USC all four years. The pay was $6.00 per game and you got to see the game. That was a great job, watching big time football.

One year, I ushered at the Rose Bowl when USC played Ohio State. That was $9.00 for the Rose Bowl game. I also worked once in a while cleaning carpets. I worked for a short time as a street cleaner on the campus at USC. I didn't last very long at that job because of the hours which were from 5:45 a.m. until 7:45 a.m. School was from eight to five, and it was just too much with all of the homework.

Another job that didn't last too long was on where I worked on files for a credit union in Los Angeles. It was fun to come across the 3x5 cards of movie stars and see how much money they had made in the 1930's and 1940's. That was before computers. It was a temporary job that we completed.

I was a custodian at a wool-weaving factory for a while. It was difficult to work much because school had become so demanding with classes going from eight to five and the accompanying homework. This was especially true during the first two years. After school, during my second and third year, I had to take care of Mark while Pearl worked.

During Christmas vacations my third and fourth year, I worked at the post office. One year I worked in the extremely large, main Los Angeles Post Office sorting mail. The next year, I delivered mail. I liked delivering mail, which was also an interesting experience because my mail route was in the ghetto area where only black people lived. I never saw a white person all day. People were very nice. Getting Christmas mail is always a pleasant experience. It was strange to be the only white person in a total black area. It gave me some real insight as to what it would be like to be a black person and raised in an area like Salt Lake, where there were so few black people.

Another interesting job that I had was to cater Jewish weddings and parties. This lasted a few months. I mainly set up, washed dishes, and then cleaned up. My last year in dental school, I worked at the Orowheat Bakery, wrapping bread. I worked about eighteen to twenty hours per week. The hours were usually from six p.m. to midnight or one a.m., three days a week.

After Sue was born, Pearl stopped working and stayed home. We sold my car and Pearl's parents helped us by paying for our rent for seven months. That was the only help that we ever received in dental school. In some respects, the years in dental school were the best of times and also the worst of times.

We went to eat out only one time in the four years during dental school, and that was at a drive-in. Pearl's Uncle Al Trauffer, from San Francisco took us to dinner once at a nice restaurant. We didn't have money except for the bare necessities. Student loans and grants were not available at that time. Over half of my classmates came from families where the dad was a physician or dentist. We basically had to make it on our own.

When I graduated with the DDS degree, we didn't have any debt. Oh happy day, we had made it! It was a great feeling to have achieved that goal. It was a real struggle, but the reward has been worth it.

I was a consultant at Wyoming State Hospital in Evanston and had a small practice in Evanston for two years. Eventually I got busy enough to transfer the patients to Salt Lake City. I considered opening a satellite office in Park City for a number of years, but life was too busy and I never got around to it. It would have been a good thing to sell the Holladay practice and go part time in Park City, especially because Sue and Scott were living there.

Park City had grown a great deal. It also would have been a good opportunity for extra retirement funds. Most of all orthodontists have two offices now. Looking back, it worked out fine with one office.

The Golden Years

I believe that life is generally what you make of it. Everyone has ups and downs. As far as golden years, I think that all of the years have "golden moments." I believe that when your children are still living at home and growing up, those are very special golden years. In general, I believe the term "golden years" generally refers to retirement years that are carefree times.

In my case, since retiring, the years have been golden. Pearl and I have the freedom to pick and choose what we want to do and when to do it. We have good health and financial security. We never had a honeymoon when we were first married, so I tell people that we are now having our honeymoon. Church has always been one of the most important aspects of our life. It has given us an anchor to help our family. The scriptures and church leaders have given important guidance and counsel. It is hard to imagine what life would be like without that help. Pearl has held about every job that you can have in the church and has always done a super job. I truly don't know anyone who has a better track record or worked harder than Pearl.

She has given so much service to others. I haven't heard of anyone who has babysat for neighbors, who weren't members of our church, for a half day, a week, or for years just to help out. People don't know much about Pearl's service. Pearl didn't want people to know. She also babysat once a week for five years for a family that had a child who needed extra help.

Pearl was a volunteer at the University Hospital for twenty years and has gone to Welfare Square countless times. She goes the extra mile for any job she has been given in the church. She has been a super helper to me for any calling that I have had.

I have had numerous callings in church – from Scout Master to Elders Quorum president, Bishop's counselor three times, to Bishop, and High Counsel member. Most of the time I had jobs that involved the youth. Now that Pearl and I are over seventy, our church jobs are not with the youth anymore. Times keep changing and younger people are better to work with the youth and children.

Pearl and I served for fourteen months as missionaries in the Inter City Mission in Salt Lake City. It was very interesting to work with people who had serious mental illness. These people had all been abandoned by their families, divorced, and had serious problems with drugs, alcohol, the law, jobs, health problems, and so forth. They could not function successfully in society. It gave us a better understanding of and more compassion for people with mental illness. It also gave us a real appreciation for good mental health, good families, and the importance of following the Church leaders' counsel. Pearl came up with the very successful idea of conducting a Family Home Evening each Monday. This was to feed the ward people. So, Each Monday, Pearl cooked nice meals for about forty people. It really helped the people to make friends and to know each other better.

Other Areas of service for me have been in the local and national dental societies. I was on the Board of Directors for the Salt Lake District Dental Society, I was the president of the Utah State Orthodontic Society, a member of the House of Delegates for American Association of Orthodontists, was on a National Council for the AAO, was a Rotary Club member for twenty years, worked and coached little league teams, and coached church sports programs. At present, I work with the Inner-City Missionary Program in the Salt Lake Valley helping with dental problems for people who have limited or no financial resources.

Life is very pleasant. We live a quite and modest life style. Pearl and I enjoy good health. We enjoy our Mt. Olympus 12th Ward, the people who go to Church there, and the neighbors who live close by. We travel to see our children each year and also enjoy other vacations. Our children and grandchildren visit us at least once a year. We are comfortable in our home and want for nothing that money can buy. We have financial security thanks to having a good plan and the discipline to follow it.

We had our 50th Wedding anniversary and took our entire family (children, spouses, and grandchildren) on a cruise to the Bahamas. We had to take the cruse over Christmas vacation due to every one's busy schedule. We wish all of our Children and their families lived closer to Salt Lake City so that we could see them more often.

Many of the Grandchildren are in college and live away from their homes. Many go to BYU so we see them at least once a month. At times, we also do shuttle service to and from the airport for the college kids. We usually can get most of our children and grandchildren together once a year for a trip to Lake Powell, a wedding, or a reunion somewhere. Pearl works very hard and tries to have a reunion every two years. Pearl and I go out to dinner at least once a week. We are extremely fortunate at this point in time because up to now, none of our family members have had any big problems or accidents that would cause unhappiness. Everyone is healthy, and anxiously engaged in church, school, work, sports, and other worthwhile activities.

All of our family is doing well and we are very proud of them. We are now in the great-grandparent stage of life and have four generations of men and women in our family. We love it.

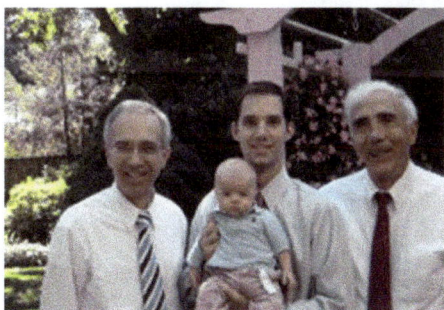

Four Generations of men, Mark, Landon, Tyler and Gus

Four Generations of women, Sue, Amy, Ellie, and Pearl

Gus G. Angelos

Present Hobbies and Activities

I played a lot of tennis for nearly thirty years. Usually, I played before work from six to seven-thirty a.m., two times a week, year round. I was a 3.5 player. I had planed to buy a ball machine and improve my game after I retired from my practice. However, my left hip started to give me trouble. I was diagnosed with mild to moderate degenerative arthritis of the left hip joint. I have backed off of tennis and play once or twice a month in the summer. I only play doubles now and have given up my plan to get a ball machine to improve my game. My body says "no."

I took up golf at age seventy-two and really enjoy that game. I hope to become a bogy golfer, but only time will tell if I achieve that goal. At least, my game is improving while most of my peer group's game is going backward, due to aging. I enjoy riding a mountain bike but don't do that as often as I would like, due to the hills around our house. I have been going to a gym almost every day for the past several years during the summer. I still enjoy water skiing and swimming. I jogged for a number of years between the ages of forty and sixty. I ran some 5K and 10K races with my son, Mark. I also ran a couple of races with Sue and Mark Young, and one or two with Scott. I didn't beat many people nor did I enjoy the jogging. I did, however enjoy the benefits of being in good shape and being with the kids.

I work out at the gym, go to the driving range, and practice golf. Skiing has always been my favorite individual sport. I loved baseball, football, and basketball, but those team sports are a thing of the past. Now I love to ski and golf.

I skied about a dozen times while in high school. I couldn't work it out to ski earlier due to finances, no car, and no one to take me. Louie Brown and I started skiing in high school when he got a car. We had some great times for a year or two before I started college. I couldn't go skiing my first three years of college due to finances. I was able to go about six times my fourth year in college. At that time, the University bought the only ski area near Laramie, Wyoming. It was called Libby Creek. I skied there for free because I was an athlete. I couldn't go skiing when I was going to dental school.

After the Army had sent me to Germany, I really wanted to get back to skiing, but was in the car accident the second time I went. That resulted in a no-skiing first year because of the broken arm.

While in Europe during the next two years, I went skiing about twelve to fifteen times. It was a wonderful experience, to ski many well-known ski areas in Switzerland, Germany, and Austria. Then another eight years went by without any skiing when we moved to Dugway, and then to California to specialize and became an Orthodontist. I finally was able to take up skiing in 1968 when we were settled in Salt Lake.

I was a low intermediate skier at that time. I was thirty-eight years old and I set a goal to go skiing fifty times a year. I was successful every year, except 1974 when I dislocated my left shoulder while skiing on Presidents Day in February with the kids.

As mentioned earlier, the children and I really had great times skiing almost every Saturday and holidays. I would also go two times during the week for about four hours each day. I was able to do this by seeing patients from 7:30 a.m. until 9:00 a.m. in the morning, rushing to the ski slope, and back to work from 2:00 p.m. until 6:00 p.m. The children and I became good recreation skiers and loved to powder ski.

After the children grew up and left home, I skied alone for a few years. Then a local TV Station, KSL, and Coca Cola Company, sponsored an easy ski race called the Coca Cola Cup. One day the race was held at the resort where I had a season pass, so I entered the race. Everyone was put in five-year age groups. The race was an easy giant slalom. I won my group that day. At the end of the season, all the weekly winners had a championship race. I got third that year. The next year I got second, and the following year, I got first place in my age group in the championships.

It was fun, and I thought I was somewhat of a ski racer. It turned out that the Coca Cola Cup was a very easy race for recreation skiers. The race was discontinued after a few years.

I found out later that I knew nothing about ski racing. I met Marv Melville through a mutual friend. Marv skied in two Winter Olympics for the U.S. in 1956 and 1960. He also coached the women's Alpine Olympic ski team in 1964. He told me about the Masters Ski racing program and invited me to go with him to a race. I went and found out I wasn't a racer at all. The Masters Ski program is the highest level of racing for older people. I came in last each time I raced, and I mean way back last. I now had a new exciting hobby be a ski racer. I was hooked.   During   the first three years, it was very difficult to get a practice course set up and to get instruction at various ski resorts. In about 1990, Park City Ski Resort started an organized Masters Ski Racing Program. Since then I have trained with an organized group of experienced coaches and ski racers.

Now that I have retired, I ski five or six days a week during the winter. There are about eighty people who train at Park City. I am the oldest. We have three coaches who take videos twice a week. Each weekday the coaches set up gates to practice for two hours. The rest of the time, we get instruction and do drills. We have a race training area that is closed to the general public. Masters Ski Races are held most every weekend in Utah, Idaho, or Wyoming. You need a license to race from the United States Ski Association and International rules are used. The races are held on Saturday and Sunday. I have never raced or skied on Sunday, so I miss many races.
This helps my competition some, but I don't mind.

I have some wonderful friends that I race against. At the end of the ski season, the National Championships are held in various resorts, mainly in the western states. I have gone to most of the National Championships races for the past fifteen years. When I started, I always finished last. Now, after fifteen years of practice, I am generally in the middle of my group. I had hoped to be one of the leaders after fifteen years, but it hasn't worked out that way. I do not know of a single competitor in my group who hasn't raced for thirty or more years. Everyone keeps getting better each year, as does the equipment.

This year I moved into the age group, seventy-five to seventy-nine year olds and did the best I ever have. My results at the National Championships held at Big Sky, Montana, are as follows: in the downhill race (which usually scares me) I got a third place. This was a miracle.

I always wanted to get a medal in a single event in the Nationals. Several years ago, I got a third place in the combined races in Alaska in the National Championships, but there were not many skiers who went to Alaska that year. This year I beat the number four man by .2 of a second. I got sixth place in the Super-G race, out of ten men in my age group. I got eighth out of thirteen men in the Giant Slalom, and sixth out of twelve men in the Slalom. There is also a combined award for the top three men who finish all the races, which I got fifth.

The combined award is figured out on a complicated point system. Every five years the World Criterion Championships are held. This race is somewhat like the Winter Olympic Ski Races held every four years. This year they were held in Sun Valley. There were 250 racers from fourteen different countries, plus another 110 racers from the USA. In these races, I got twelfth out of seventeen in the Giant Slalom. In the Criterion Giant Slalom, I got seventh out of fourteen. I got fifth out of ten in the Slalom, and eleventh in the Super G out of sixteen men. I don't know how many more years I will be healthy enough to race.

I hope to avoid any big injures or illnesses and to continue racing for quite a while because I greatly enjoy it. All of my life I have enjoyed athletic competition. I always tried to do what was best for the team and not what was best for me. I have shown good sportsmanship and have never been ejected from any game for poor sportsmanship. Rules are rules. I don't care to argue with officials. I just try to put forth my best effort and have fun.

I loved sports, especially the ones that I participated in. They shaped my life. As I have grown older, I have mellowed even more to a position in live where I "let live," as long as it doesn't hurt anyone or isn't illegal. Not that I am perfect, but I always considered myself an easy guy to get along with. I have always had many friends and got along with everyone. I tried to live the Golden Rule and not be judgmental.

How would I like to be remembered? Just as an ordinary guy who tried to do the right thing, one who loved the Lord, his family, our country, and worked for what I received. I never tried to hurt anyone or anything. Tried to conserve all resources and be self-reliant. I never expected or believed in entitlements for myself, only for people who had real needs or real handicaps.

Gus G. Angelos

186

Travels

D uring my early years, we weren't able to travel because we didn't have a car, had very few relatives, and my dad worked long hours every day. His work didn't allow any vacation time. I never dreamed of going to Europe. Baseball enabled me to travel around the USA quite a bit and to Canada two times. While in the Army, Pearl and I traveled extensively through out Western Europe. We have also traveled to Israel, Egypt, and Turkey. We have been to Greece four or five times. Pearl and I have traveled to all of the western European Countries, except Spain and Portugal. Since our Army days in Europe, we have traveled back to Europe six or seven times.

We spent two weeks in Australia and New Zealand when Scott was on his Mission. We have been to Mexico and Canada a few times. Hawaii once. We have been to Alaska twice as well as most of the fifty states. We have taken several cruise ship tours around the Caribbean, Mediterranean, and to Alaska. We have gone on several Church Tours around the country. Growing up I thought I would never travel outside the US. In those days only very rich people traveled abroad. Travel is much easier now and more affordable. Beside the cruise for our 50th wedding anniversary, we also took our four children and their spouses to Switzerland a few years ago.

In 2011 we took a wonderful river cruise trip up the Rhine River and spent a week in Switzerland with Sue's family. We travel some each year, manly to see our children and to go to Lake Powell, which we have been doing for about forty years.

Many years ago, I thought it might be fun to travel to each of the seven continents. That was probably an ego thing. I have had the good fortune to be able to travel as much as I wanted. Along life's journey, decisions and choices need to be made. I really don't have many regrets. We must do the best we can with the circumstances that exist at the time.

Health History

My mother told me I had whooping cough when I was a baby. When I was two years of age, Sam had infected tonsils. Mom told me that when the doctor came to our house for Sam's tonsillitis, he also looked at me and decided to remove both Sam's and my tonsils, which was done on the dinning room table at our house. I do not remember this. Chicken pox was the only childhood disease that I remember having at around age twelve. I think I may have had other childhood diseases, but in a mild form. I can only guess on that one.

Years later, I was concerned that I might get the mumps when our children had the mumps. Fortunately, it didn't happen. Occasionally I would get a cold and I had the flu once when I was in my early teens. I had a light case of pneumonia when I was about fifteen years old. It was unusual for me to miss a day of school due to illness. It has been rare for me to have headaches or stomachaches in my life.

I believe I have been very fortunate to have a good immune system and good heredity. In my early years, my biggest health problem was hay fever. It was chronic and year round. It was diagnosed when I was about age twelve years. I would snore at night and was a mouth breather. Hay fever caused the mucous membrane of my nose to enlarge and secrete mucous continuously. I had some de-sensitizing shots for a few months at age twelve, and I was also given an antihistamine that helped. I took that antihistamine at bedtime for several years until the manufacture stopped producing it.

After becoming a dentist, I gave myself desensitizing shots for hay fever for about twenty years, which was a great help. I also had three minor surgeries to enlarge the air passages of my nose and remove some of the excess mucous membrane. I broke my nose playing football at about age twelve, and I had an operation at age twenty-one, which straightened the septum and changed the shape of my nose. I can now breathe through my nose quite well. My nose runs quicker, and more in cold weather, than anyone I have ever seen. This is an embarrassment at times when skiing, but I put up with it.

During my teen years, I was embarrassed because in the evening time my nose would become so obstructed that my voice would have a very nasal sound. It sounded as if I were pinching my nose when speaking and I didn't like that. To this day I still think I have a monotone and somewhat nasal tone when speaking.

During my teenage years, I thought it would be fun to be a sports broadcaster. When I first heard a recording of my voice in high school, I quickly decided I would never make it as a sportscaster.

I have had several broken bones. My nose at about age twelve, my right arm in three places at age twenty-eight, three ribs snow skiing at about age sixty-three, and one rib water skiing at about age sixty-five. I dislocated my left shoulder while snow skiing at age forty-five. I also broke the tendon in my left thumb skiing at the age of seventy-four. I tore the ACL in my right knee playing basketball at about age forty-five and have had both knees scoped for torn cartilage during the past fifteen years.

I have had surgical operations for my broken arm, knees, a hernia repair, nose, thumb, and prostate surgery to remove a cancerous prostate gland in 1992. The ACL was rebuilt in my right knee in 1999. I missed only 1 day in eight years of college due to illness when I had the twenty-four hour flu. I missed two days of work due to a cold when I was in the Army. I never missed one day of work in private practice due to accident or illness. I did miss one afternoon and had to cancel patients once, when I was skiing at Solitude and an avalanche blocked the road for a few hours so that I couldn't go back to work. I scheduled time off for any surgery. I just toughed it out if I didn't feel good or was injured.

I have also been very lucky to have very few headaches, upset stomachs, colds, aches or pains, or any health problems. I have had high cholesterol for forty years. The cholesterol usually measured in the 220's. About 1995 the doctor prescribed Zocor, 10 milligrams per day, and now the cholesterol is around 165.

An Autobiography

My right hip bone hurts some after I play tennis and the Doctor diagnosed it as mild to moderate hip joint degeneration. (Update) My right hip was replaced in April 2012. This worked out wonderfully. Eight weeks after the surgery the doctor told me I could do anything I wanted. Now I have no pain, more range of motion, and the hip is stronger than before.

My hearing has gradually declined over a thirty-year period, starting in my late forties. I took several hearing tests during this time and was told there was nothing I could do to prevent the decline. This seems to be a hereditary condition common in my mother's family. I never did abuse my ears with loud noises or injuries. I have been wearing hearing aids since the age of sixty-nine. My eyes are still very good, which again seems to be a trait from my mother's family. I passed the eye exam for a driver's license two years ago, but my eyesight is getting a little poorer, especially the left eye for distance vision.

In 2004 the ophthalmologist told me I have the beginning of a cataract in the left eye. I never did wear glasses for dentistry except for protection. During my last few years in practice, I used optical loops once in a while. (Update) I had cataract surgery for the left eye in 2009 with a good result. I still don't wear glasses, but the close vision is getting more difficult.

My blood pressure is usually around 100-110 over 60-70. My primary care physician tells me I am healthy and doing everything right. I always had a lot of exercise as it made me feel better mentally as well as physically. I have always eaten a good diet with lots of fruits and vegetables. I cut back on red meat, as I got older. I eat more poultry and fish now. I eat too many sweets.

I usually sleep eight hours at night and get up early. My brother Sam had bypass heart surgery at age seventy-four. Both my sister and mother had a bundle branch block in their hearts and both took medication for it. My brother and sister are in good health otherwise.

My father's death certificate says he died from congestive heart failure and that he had hardening of the arteries and plaque built up, narrowing the arteries. His lungs were very poor due to fifty years of smoking. Dad's death at age sixty-seven years was typical of congestive heart failure. My mother died at age eighty-five. She had dementia the last three years of her life and didn't recognize any of her children. She was always pleasant and easy to take care of. The death certificate lists mom's death as from pneumonia. My sister kept her in her home the last four years. Because mom couldn't remember anything, I thought it would be okay to put her in a rest home. Margaret wouldn't hear of it, and took marvelous, loving care of our mom. I can never thank her enough. I had to insist that Margaret accept money for the outstanding care she gave our mother. Margaret's husband, Bob Forsgren was also very loving and helpful with Mom for which I am grateful.

Both my parents had hernia repairs. My dad had a diet high in red meat and had high cholesterol. Neither of my parents exercised much in their adult life. My dad had one brother and one sister who lived past ninety years. The rest of his siblings died in their middle sixties from heart problems. Mom also had high cholesterol, however the doctor did not put her on any medication that I know of. My mother had a half-brother, Fred, who died of alcoholism at about age forty-four. The other two half-siblings died in their eighties. I do not know the cause of their deaths.

My grandmother Bertha was killed in an auto accident at age seventy-five but was in good health as far as I know. I know nothing of my mother's biological father. My great grandmother Matern died at age ninety-four. My great grandfather Matern died from cancer in his sixties. I do not know what type of cancer. Birthdates, death, and locations for my family, along with Pearl's family, are on our genealogy sheets. There is a history of heart disease on my father's side of the family. I have no knowledge of high blood pressure or strokes on my dad's or mother's side of the family. Other than my great grandfather on my mother's side, I do not know of anyone else who died of cancer. I do not know of any diabetes, Alzheimer's, Parkinson disease, Downs Syndrome, birth defects, Cystic Fibrosis, or obesity in my family. As far as eye disease, I don't know of any glaucoma problems.

I think my mother had macular degeneration problems. She could see quite well until her death. Almost all of the blood relatives have worn eyeglasses as they've gotten older. My mother's family seems to have good eyes and poor hearing. I know of no family history of depression or any mental illness. Both of my parents, my brother, and my sister, and I, all have high cholesterol. The only medication I take is one cholesterol tablet and one 45 mg Iron tablet each day. The iron tablet is for angiodysplasia of the colon and small intestine. Angiodysplasia is a condition that causes a small amount of bleeding from pimple-like lesions. The cause is unknown. There is no treatment except to replace the iron loss each day. It is not precancerous.

I also take multivitamins. My mother had a miscarriage, as did my daughter, Sue. Keep in mind that I did not have the good fortune to know many of my relatives so this health history is shallow and incomplete.

As to my mouth, it has been a big problem to me all my life. The hay fever and mouth breathing caused my jawbones to grow in an abnormal way, typical for mouth breathers. The gum tissues of my mouth have not been as firm and healthy as is normal for one who takes good care of the mouth. I have seen a periodontist for fifty years on a regular basis, and have taken very good care of my mouth since deciding to become a dentist. My teeth were too large for the jawbones and as a result, were very crowded. I have had seven teeth (plus the one tooth that was removed at age twelve) removed – a total of eight teeth – for the two orthodontic treatments. My first orthodontic treatment was at age twenty-one, and the other time was at age forty-five years. I have had about fifteen different gum surgeries. I have ten teeth with root canal fillings. I could go on in detail, but suffice to say, ever since the time I started dental school, I have taken excellent care of my mouth. I still have most of my teeth but my mouth requires more daily care that average. I have three posterior bridges of three units each. I have several root canals and four implants to date.

I do not have the strength, speed, endurance, or balance that I had as a young man. As a person in his seventies, I compare very well physically to my age group. I still like competition and ski race actively in the alpine masters program. I play tennis but not as often as I used to. I water ski and have taken up golf, which I enjoy a great deal. I go to the gym when not skiing almost every day. I take bike rides on occasion and hikes once in a while. (Update, I gave up tennis at about age seventy-five) I am more than two inches shorter than I was when I was in my twenties. I now weigh 175 pounds. I cannot run very fast, but am happy to be able to run even a little. I learned at a young age you do the best you can with what you've got. Like most people who participate in athletics, I would like to have been taller, stronger, and faster, but have always been thankful for the gifts that the Lord blessed me with and the good they brought into my life.

Summary

All things considered, I have had a wonderful life. Early in life, I developed a thirst for knowledge, a love for sports competition, and a love for life in general. I could never have asked for more in life than I have been blessed with, starting with the most important thing in the world – my family.

I hope that when the time comes to leave this mortal life, it will be quick and I will not be a burden to anyone. I hope that my family will look upon my passing through the veil as a happy occasion of me going home. As mentioned before, I would like to be remembered as a grateful, happy, ordinary guy who followed his dreams, worked hard, and tried to give life his best shot – someone who loved the Lord, his family, his church, the good old USA, and enjoyed a very long, happy, and good life.

My advice to any family member who reads this memoir is to stay true to yourself, your family, and the Church. Be the best you can be in all things. Keep the commandments and covenants you make. Keep the Ten Commandments and live the Golden Rule. Stay close to the spirit so you can receive inspiration and make good decisions. Have a good work ethic. Be a good example. Be slow to anger and careful when making judgments. Be kind to everyone, including animals, and especially your family. Conserve and take care of the planet. Know that life has some bumps along the way as well as some beautiful sunsets. Live a healthy lifestyle and enjoy the good things that are here for us. Look for the good in all people and things. Laugh and be happy every day. Be thankful for the opportunities and blessings and gifts you receive from the Lord.

The Church is true. God bless you all.

Gus G. Angelos

Addendum

Update of an unpleasant experience: On February 2, 2006, I went skiing for my fifty-sixth time that year and was getting ready for some important Western Regionals races that were being held at Park City. I took a timed trial run for the Super-G race. On my way down the hill after the timed run, I heard a big noise when someone ran over the back of my skis and hit me. I think it was a snow boarder. I had my helmet on but still sustain a serious head injury. I had a subdural hematoma, which consisted of three blood clots plus a bruised area in my brain. I wanted to keep skiing, but my friend Marv Melville said I should go home. I always listened to Marv, because he knows almost everything there is to know about ski racing. I don't remember driving home from Park City, or much about the accident.

Later that afternoon, my headache got worse. I phoned Mark Angelos and he said I should go to the emergency room and check it out. At the hospital ER, they took a cat scan, saw the extent of the injury, and hospitalized me. I was in the hospital for a week, and then came home. I remember very little about the week in the hospital or the first three weeks at home. Evidently, I answered all the questions correctly and appeared okay the next morning after the accident, so they were ready to send me home. Then I had a seizure in the hospital and that changed everything. Ten different doctors have taken care of me. The law prohibits anyone to drive a car for three months after seizures. The doctors told me that I could not do a lot of things for three months. After I got home from the hospital, I remember only bits and pieces of what went on for three weeks.

About three weeks after the accident, I discovered my right leg was swollen, and I immediately went to see the doctor. The ultrasound showed a blood clot in my right leg below the knee. The doctor decided to immediately put a filter in the vein by the lung in case the blood clot broke loose and moved into my lungs. The filter was placed and four weeks later, I was prepped to remove it. Another ultrasound was taken and it showed the blood clot still present in the leg. Another appointment was scheduled four weeks later to remove the filter. The next ultrasound showed the blood clot had broken loose and was captured by the filter. So much time went by that the doctor decided that the filter would have to stay because scar tissue would make it difficult to remove. So I will always have it. The blood clot in the leg might have been dissolved with blood thinners early on. However, I could not be put on blood thinners until the brain injury had completely healed. I am very lucky because if a blood clot gets into the lungs, it can be fatal.

The whole experience left me weak and I did not have much energy. Pearl had to drive me every place I needed to go for three months. She really was a good nurse and took good care of me. She is a sweetheart.

I started going to the gym because I wanted to get back into shape. Complete inactivity at an old age isn't good for the body. I found I got tired very easy and had lost some of my equilibrium. I thought everything was moving too slow and went back to see the doctor. I told the doctor that I thought I was going backward, inasmuch as my strength and endurance were getting worse rather than better. Blood tests confirmed that I was severely anemic, and the loss of iron had also caused the red blood cells to get smaller.

Tomorrow, June 30, 2006, I am scheduled to get a colonoscopy and endoscopy. The doctor needs to find out what is causing the anemia. I think it is probably due to the head injury and the blood thinners I have been taking. It has been a terrible experience for me and shows how life can change in a minute.

<u>Update on November 2006:</u> The tests could not confirm where the blood loss was coming from. Nothing showed in the urine or stools. I was put on iron and vitamin pills for six weeks and was removed from all other medication. Follow up lab tests confirmed that the blood chemistry was back to normal. I have continued to exercise at a gym and be active. I believe I am now back to normal and I feel wonderful.

Update in February 2007: A good ski buddy and friend is a cardiologist named Rodney Badger. We have been friends for many years. I told him I still didn't have the energy I should have. He said he would check my heart and lungs, as this could be the source of the problem. Rod ordered several tests, including a treadmill test and echogram, as well as many other tests. These all proved negative – I have a good heart and no constricted arteries. I asked him to check the blood that had been drawn for one of the tests. It showed I was anemic again. The hemoglobin was at 8, which is classified as severe anemia.

Dr. Cris Romney, my primary doctor, is now trying to find the cause of the anemia. I am back taking iron pills. I am told it will take a couple of months to build up the blood iron. Dr. Romney arranged for another test in which I swallowed a very large pill. I had an apparatus on my waist, which I think was a miniature camera. It took 200 pictures of my digestive tract. Finally, the diagnosis was made that I have angiodysplasia of the colon and small intestine. There is no known cause for the small pimple like lesions, and they are not precancerous. They cause a slight amount of bleeding which takes iron from the blood. I take one iron pill a day, which replaces the iron I loose, and I am feeling normal again.

My latest check-up in September 2008 showed everything normal and I feel good. I rarely have a day when I don't feel good.

During my stay in the hospital one of the monitoring machines kept flashing sleep apnea. After being released from the hospital, I consulted with a doctor and took an overnight sleep test in the hospital. I was diagnosed with severe sleep apnea and was put on a CPAP sleeping machine. CPAP stands for constant positive air pressure. Later follow up treatment showed that I had Central Sleep Apnea rather than Obstructive Sleep Apnea. So I now wear a VPAP sleeping machine. V stands for variable positive air pressure. I now sleep with the VPAP machine.

<u>Update from September 2010:</u> Blood chemistry and physical exam shows everything normal. I still take accordion lessons. Pearl and I just started to see a personal trainer together. It should help me with posture, flexibility, and increase some muscle strength, or at least slow down the aging factor. I go to the gym four or five times a week, except during ski season. We have a fun busy life, are both happy, and quite healthy.

<u>Update June 2012:</u> I still haven't finished my life story. I am presently adding pictures to the story. Midway through the ski season, my right hip started to hurt a lot. I got a cortisone shot that was like a magic bullet. It lasted to the end of the ski season, at which time I had an artificial right hip replacement done. The hip surgery was very successful and I was back to full activity in eight weeks. I am sorry to repeat things in this long life story. I also apologize for any errors.

I had a good ski season in 2011-12. I had hoped to do well at the National Championships because they were held in Park City. I was disappointed. In the four races, I got fourth and sixth place, and fell on the other two races. There were only seven men in my age group from various areas around the USA. I plan to take a year away from racing and just enjoy free skiing. My goal is still to ski 100 times. In the last few years, I only have the energy to ski a half-day, but I love the mountains, trees, skiing, and etc.

Sue and Mark Young have been in Oregon the past year as the Mission President and Mission Mom. We really miss them and will be glad when they return in two years. They are doing a great job and working hard.

I quit taking accordion lessons – just lost interest for the time being. Pearl and I still have a fun busy life and are happy and healthy.

<u>Health update:</u> In June 2012, I started noticing some shortness of breath and edema (water retention) in my lower legs. This came about very quickly with no previous history. After consulting five doctors (and taking about ten lab tests, including a tread mill test, an MRI, a heart muscle biopsy, and bone marrow biopsy), I was diagnosed with amyloidosis, which causes congestive heart failure. Amyloidosis is a rare blood disorder that deposits a protein in ones organs, mainly the kidneys and heart. In my case my heart muscle has thickened and doesn't pump enough blood for normal or vigorous activity. There is more than one type of amyloidosis and fortunately for me I have a more mild type.

The first diagnosis from a local lab was a severe type of amyloidosis, which is fatal within a year or two. The lab results from Mayo Brothers Hospital showed a milder type of amyloidosis. Only the symptoms of amyloidosis can be treated, which means I take a diuretic and potassium pill daily. I can exercise all I want, but do not have much endurance. I just get out of breath easily. I can ski, walk nine holes of golf, and go to the gym so I am happy.

I am okay with this condition, as I would prefer to die from heart disease rather than other causes. No one wants to be a vegetable or have your mind give out so you become a burden to your family or society. The doctors tell me I will survive a few more years and still be pretty active. Amyloidosis is not a genetic thing or cancerous.

Gus G. Angelos

Health update 2014: It has been two years since I was diagnosed with Senile Cardiac Amyloidosis. I have read there are thirty-six amyloid proteins that are associated with human disease. I needed a pace maker about a year ago. I also had atrial arrhythmia and had a cardio-version procedure, which worked out well. I have noticed a gradual decline in my endurance and run out of breath quicker than a year ago.

I had a good ski season at Deer Valley the past year and skied ninety-six times. I only ski for a half day. I go early in the morning before it gets crowded and while the snow is still easy to ski – maybe catch some powder. I cannot ski the powder or groomed snow like I could years ago. Never the less, I am looking forward to another good ski season.

I stopped water skiing this year and have to face the fact that I am an old man. I focus and am happy to do what I can do. Believe it or not, my golf game is improving. Last week I shot a 47 and 42 for nine holes. I still have the hope to shoot my age and maybe get a hole in one.

In summary, I am a happy person who enjoys the good things that Pearl and I can do: Church, family get-togethers, parties, limited travel, reading, going to the gym, skiing, golfing, and watching our two new TV's. We haven't been to the movies for years, due to my hearing problem. In truth, there aren't many new movies that interest me. I like DVD movies because they usually have captions. I also like TV educational programs and sports, mainly college football, baseball, and ski racing.

I now take short nap three or four times a week, and do very little yard work. I never did enjoy yard work. I admire people to do. It is good exercise for older people as well as a peaceful activity for the mind.

Family activities are still the best. The past few months I have reflected and pondered upon life, its meanings, and how blessed I have been. The following are some of my thoughts: I believe generally older people look back on their life and realize the most important thing is one's family and friends. Surveys overwhelmingly say terminally ill people when asked wish they had spent more time with their family.

How you treated other people and how you were treated is paramount to one's happiness and peace of mind. I think older people generally become more forgiving and less judgmental and know that material things, positions held, or most accomplishments aren't as

204

important as they once were. I also believe that one's faith or religion has a lot to do with how happy you are in your senior years.

As you get to your older years, life is usually less stressful. You have time to "smell the roses" and do things you were too busy to do earlier in life. Older people become more set in their ways and often resist changes in their routines. Many times it becomes hard to make a decision that gets you out of your comfort zone.

I also think we become more conservative. One just doesn't have the energy or desire to do as many things that one did during youth and earlier years. This is accompanied by a decline both physically and mentally. Usually there are some aches and pains that come with old age.

All of us are different and have had different life experiences. I have always been active physically. That – along with my life style, good luck, and very importantly a good family – has made it possible for me to have a wonderful rich and happy long life. It is nice to have piece of mind and be happy.

Pearl and I are both over eighty years of age and still functioning pretty good. We are happy and as busy as we want to be. I believe the Lord wants all his children to be successful and happy. Parents also want this. If we could all keep the Commandments and live the Golden Rule, life would be much better for everyone.

Thank goodness for my great family. Our four children were married in the Salt Lake Temple and by their wonderful Grandfather Walt Trauffer. So far all of my grandchildren, who are married, were married in the temple as well. This has made Pearl and me very happy. At this point in time, all my children and grandchildren are doing very well with their lives. I couldn't ask for more.

I don't know how much longer I will live. This is probably as good as any place to end my life story. I sincerely hope that after reading through so many pages, it has been worth your time and that there is something within these pages that might help you as you travel along your life journey.

Pearl and I have paid for our funerals. We will be buried at Wasatch Lawn Cemetery in Salt Lake City. It is interesting to me that we don't seem to have much free agency when it comes to passing through the veil to the other side. I certainly don't want to be a burden to anyone and hope the end of my life experience will be quick. When I get there, I think that experience will be awesome and like going home to loved ones.

Reglion

I was baptized in was the Greek Orthodox Church as an infant. We were not a church-going family. Once or twice a year I would be taken to the Greek Orthodox Church by Sam's godfather. Occasionally I was sent to Harvard Ward (LDS Church) when I was young. I was fortunate to grow up in Salt Lake City and have lots of friends. Most of them were LDS. However, we didn't talk about religion, and most of my closest friends did not attend church. I wrote earlier about the LDS Scout and Basketball programs and my participation.

Living away from Salt Lake during the summer when I was age seventeen and eighteen, and my association with older, war-experienced men, opened my mind in many areas. During that time, occasionally I would go to the Catholic church or different Protestant churches with ball player friends when the games were away from Salt Lake. The games were at night and there was not much to do during the day.

Pearl and her great family were a wonderful example to me. Pearl, in a quiet way, gave me lots of encouragement. In my early years, church and religion were not part of my life. I just didn't think of those things. As I got older and matured, I started to think about deeper things in life. While I was in college, I decided I needed more religion in my life. I started going to the LDS Institute on a pretty regular basis during my third year at the University of Wyoming. After Pearl and I got married we went 100% of the time.

I didn't have any strong religious beliefs or questions when growing up, but some started in college. Mormon doctrine always made more sense and answered my questions better than anything I had heard in other churches. Pearl was a big factor, and let me know from 'day one' that when she got married, it would be in the Mormon temple.

Testimony

My testimony and knowledge grew slowly throughout my early years. I wished I would have taken seminary and institute classes when I was a full-time student. My testimony and knowledge has continued to grow during my lifetime. Looking back in time as an old man, I wish I had been raised in the LDS church and learned the things that are taught, starting with Primary. I wish I had gone a Mission as a young man. I now have a very strong testimony of the truthfulness of the LDS church and its teachings.

I know the gospel needed to be restored on the earth. I know that Joseph Smith was a prophet and was instrumental in restoring God's church to the earth. I know that the Book of Mormon is true as well as the Doctrine and Covenants and Pearl of Great Price. I know we have a living prophet today, who happens to be Thomas S. Monson. I am proud to be a member of this Church.

I know that Jesus Christ is the Head of this Church and that we will be judged fairly by the Savior. We are here on this earth to gain a mortal body, gain experiences, and be tested. I know that the Lord loves us and wants us all to happy and successful during our sojourn on the earth. I am extremely grateful for the Atonement that was made on our behalf.

I know the Lord wants us all to be happy and to be obedient and live the gospel. He is willing to forgive us, help us to do the right things, and has given us a plan of salvation. I believe that the life hereafter will be a wonderful life where I look forward to seeing my parents and other family members and friends.

I know that this country was preserved for the restoration of the gospel. I love the Lord, my family, the Church, and this country with all my heart.

God bless you.

All the Bishops of our Ward from the time it was organized until the time the Stake combined and everything was changed. Gus is on back row second from left.

Last photo of entire family. Grandma Trauffer's funeral April 2003

Probably the last family reunion we will ever have. Oregon, 2013. Pearl and I with yellow shirts. Mark A's family in red, Sue's family in light blue/green, Scott's family in orange, and Craig's family in dark blue in the top row. Only Bryant and Mary Angelos were not present. Their new baby was born the week of the reunion. Blaine Baker was in dental school and not present. Everyone had a wonderful time.

127 Harvard Ave. Only house I lived at until I grew up and left home. House was bought in 1931 and sold in about 1990. Photo about 1947

Sam's first bike & me -Note our house left of Sam

Last Update August 2015

My health is gradually declining. I get winded quickly and become breathless. I must rest more often. One flight of steps requires me to rest. Also walking fifty to 100 steps makes it necessary to stop to catch my breath. The doctors tell me I am at stage-C, as far as Heart Failure classification.

I did get up to ski seventy-five times last season, but had to stop more often coming down the hill. My skill level is dropping off and I am afraid I will not be able to ski this season. It is hard to give up something that I love so much.

My golf game (riding nine holes) is still improving a little, which makes me happy. Pearl is in good health but has macular degeneration. She cannot drive at night and stays off the freeways. Pearl is really helping me a great deal in every way possible these days. My hearing problem causes me to miss a lot of conversation and the church class discussions.

The sleep doctor put me on a new sleep apnea machine, which is working out good and includes oxygen at night.

Most importantly, all of the family is doing well. We now have sixteen beautiful great-grandchildren, who are spread over the entire USA.

Pearl and I have a nice life without many obligations or worries. We can use Facebook to stay in touch with lots of our family. Our travels are small, but we are very happy just hanging out and being together.

Church and the temple are very important. We have a small group of close friends and don't lack for anything. Sue and Mark Young and their boys all live close by and they do a very good job looking after us.

All in all life is good. I never could have asked for a better family or life. This is probably as good of time to end my life story.

A last few words

Health wise, I am still going downhill. I cannot golf anymore and have had to quit doing sealings at the temple. I am getting pretty much housebound. I inwardly feel I am letting people down by not making any real contribution anywhere. Yesterday, the bishop and High Priest group leader came by. I was released as a home teacher.

Yesterday, I was also put on hospice, which will make life easier. My care will be mainly at home. Overall, I have done what I could do and not having been terminally ill before, I will just ride things out and see where it all goes. Thanks for your time and I hope each of you who read this, will strive to be the best you can be during the mortal time you are given to live on this earth.

~ Gus George Angelos